# Profit from productivity

**PICSIE BOOKS**
P.O. Box 786340
Sandton 2146
Tel (011) 442-8175

FIONA HALSE
JOHN HUMPHREY

# Profit from productivity

JUTA & CO, LTD
Cape Town · Wetton · Johannesburg

First Published in 1986
Second impression 1990

© Juta & Co, Ltd, 1986
P.O. Box 123, Kenwyn 7790

ISBN 0 7021 1707 2

Set in 10 on 12pt Times and printed on
80 g/m² Mondi Classic Antique

Set, printed and bound in the Republic
of South Africa by Creda Press,
Solan Road, Cape Town

# Contents

# Foreword

Our aim in producing this book is to provide managers, supervisors, and trainers with a basic understanding of how to improve productivity in any business organisation.

We wanted to give it a provocative title like "One-minute productivity", or "In search of productivity", but we couldn't get it all into one minute and you don't need to search for opportunities for productivity improvement — they exist in every work situation.

We have tried to keep it simple and practical so that it will not only suggest a basic method to higher management but also be used as a training aid down to supervisory level. It is not intended to turn you into a Work Study expert but if it arouses your interest in the subject there are several excellent text-books you can turn to if you want to hone your skills.

Improving productivity is not only necessary to our economic survival, it also provides a new and absorbing dimension to your job — a constant challenge to do it better.

So let's get down to it without wasting any more of your valuable productive time . . .

# What is productivity?

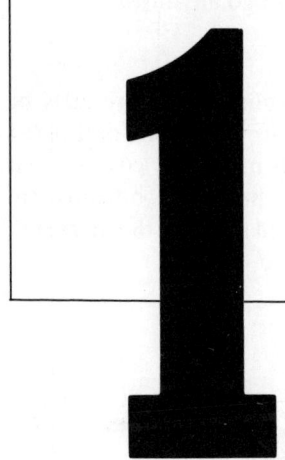

Well, for a start, it isn't half the things that people (who should know better) say it is. It does not mean

- working harder — unless people are loafing on the job;
- cutting costs — unless this can be done without affecting quality;
- reducing staff and workers unless your market is shrinking;
- extra work for managers — it's part of their job;
- employing specialists — it's a job for everyone.

There is nothing new about productivity. Early writings on the subject go as far back as 400 BC and by AD 1400 an efficient assembly line was working in Venice. By the 1800's the role of the worker in productivity had been recognised but it was not until the early 1900's that the modern approach to the productivity of industrial processes really came into being.

In South Africa its importance began to be recognised in 1967 which saw the creation of the National Productivity Institute — a joint venture by Government and private enterprise to create awareness of the need for productivity improvement. However little real progress was made until the onset of the economic recession in 1983. Since then the word "productivity" has become the best-used (and abused) word in the manager's vocabulary.

Many people confuse production and productivity. Whilst both are important to any business they are really quite different in meaning. So let's clear up this misunderstanding before we go any further.

**Production**

Production is the process of converting resources into products or services. It is usually measured in terms of output per time period (eg boxes per hour, tonnes per day, bookings per month) or cost per unit of output (eg R10 per box, R20 per ton, etc). The objective of production operations is to meet the forecasted needs of the market in which they perform at the lowest possible cost.

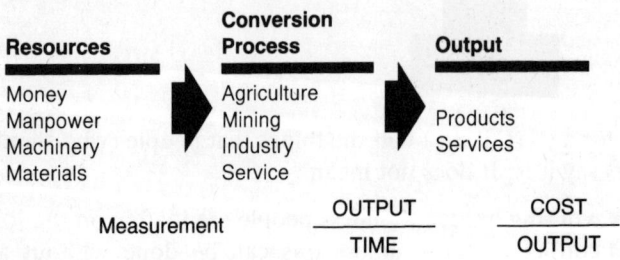

The output of a production process can be improved by increasing the input of resources or by changing the process or both.

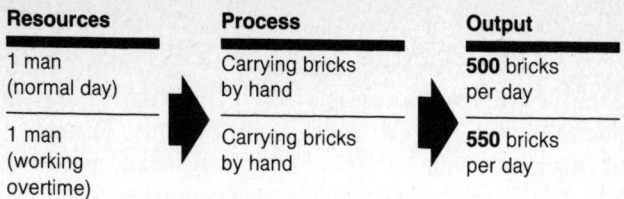

| Resources | Process | Output |
|---|---|---|
| 1 man (normal day) | Carrying bricks by hand | **500** bricks per day |
| 1 man (working overtime) | Carrying bricks by hand | **550** bricks per day |

If we increase the resources by making a worker work overtime we will increase the output of the process and so meet our market needs. However we may not have improved our costs in doing so.

| Resources | Cost | Input | Output | Cost of Output |
|---|---|---|---|---|
| 1 man × 8 hrs @ R2 per hour | R16 | **R16** | 500 bricks | **3,2c** per brick |
| 1 man × 8 hrs @ R2 per hour and 2 hrs OT @ R2,50 per hr. | R16 R5 | **R21** | 550 bricks | **3,8c** per brick (increase 19%) |

If we can modify the process to enable the man to produce more without working harder or longer we may be able to meet our target and reduce the cost of output as well.

| Resources | Cost | Input | Output | Cost of Output |
|---|---|---|---|---|
| 1 man × 8 hrs @ R2 per hour | R16 | **R24** | 800 bricks | **3c** per brick |
| 1 wheelbarrow @ R1 per hour | R8 | | (increase 60%) | (reduction 6%) |

By adding to the resources and changing the process we have increased production by 60% and reduced the unit costs by 6%. That's what productivity is all about.

3

## Service operations

In our examples so far we have tended to concentrate on the more traditional conversion processes which occur in agriculture, mining or manufacturing industry and which, until recently, formed the major part of business revenue. Today they have been overtaken by the service industry which, in some Western countries, forms as much as 80% of all industry.

Service operations make use of resources to create products just the same as does manufacturing industry although frequently the product is hard to visualise. Airlines, hotels, markets, chemist shops and garages are all examples of service operations which use manpower, machinery, materials and money to create a product or products which meet the needs of their customers.

> When you arrive safely and comfortably at your destination your flight has been the product of a process which buys airplanes, maintains them, trains people to fly them and provide in-flight service, uses millions of units of fuel, food and toilet paper, and handles millions of items of baggage. The production of an airline can be measured in "Passenger/miles" and the cost and contribution of each resource can be similarly measured.

Exactly the same principles apply to the service divisions of a company such as personnel, finance and marketing. The product they produce must be defined and the resources involved must be used effectively. It is no more difficult to measure the output of an accounts clerk than a machine operator as we will show you later. Both have a contribution to make to the productivity of the company.

## Productivity

Productivity is simply a measure of the ratio between the output of a process and the input of resources needed for it. It is usually expressed as output divided by input.

$$Productivity = \frac{\text{OUTPUT}}{\text{INPUT}}$$

Output can be expressed in terms of units or volume (eg tonnes, litres, boxes, etc) and these units have usually been already determined for production planning purposes. In cases where outputs cannot be individually defined a monetary total can be used (eg Rands of production, Rands of sales, etc).

Inputs are usually separated into Manpower, Machinery and Materials. In cases where inputs cannot be segregated a monetary value can be substituted (eg Rands of material).

| Input | Unit of measurement |
|---|---|
| Manpower | per manhour |
| Machinery | per machine hour |
| Materials | per material unit |
| Money | per Rand of input |

The most commonly used measure of productivity is Manpower and it is the one usually referred to in the press when comparing our productivity with that of other countries. However, since manpower often forms a relatively low component of the total cost of a product it is vital to consider the productivity of all resource inputs when studying the productivity of a process.

In a large printing operation the relative costs of inputs expressed as a percentage of total direct costs were

| | |
|---|---|
| Manpower | 25% |
| Materials | 40% |
| Machinery | 35% |

A newly-appointed manager considered the operation overstaffed and, after a long and damaging conflict with the works union, succeeded in reducing the labour by 10% thus reducing overall costs by 2,5% for which he was warmly congratulated by the Board.

However, both the manager and the Board apparently overlooked the fact that materials wasted and spoiled in the process amounted to 10% (or 4% of total costs), whilst set-up and cleaning time on the presses amounted to 30% of machine time (10,5% of total costs).

If the manager had devoted the same energy to improving the productivity of materials and machinery by reducing wastage and down-time by at least 50% as he had done in reducing labour he would have reduced total costs by more than 7% without running the risk of costly labour stoppages.

The term "machinery" is used to cover all the machines, equipment and transport used in the process. Similarly "materials" is used to cover not only raw or semi-finished materials but also power, light, steam and other utilities consumed.

**Improving Productivity**

The cost of any product or service is the sum of the costs of the resources used in producing it. The more productive each of those resources can be made the lower the final cost of the product. In a free market the lower the cost of a product, the greater the demand it generates and the more profitable the enterprise, with ultimately a beneficial effect on the living standards of everyone.

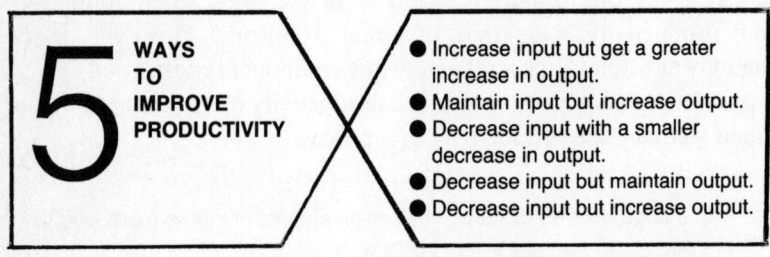

5 WAYS TO IMPROVE PRODUCTIVITY

● Increase input but get a greater increase in output.
● Maintain input but increase output.
● Decrease input with a smaller decrease in output.
● Decrease input but maintain output.
● Decrease input but increase output.

In a factory making domestic appliances the assembly operation for household fans comprised three workers. One attached the rotating mechanism to the base; one attached the motor and threaded the flex through the base; one fitted the fan blades and guard assembly. The complete fan then went off to the inspection department. The work was monotonous, labour turnover high and the number of rejects which had to be re-worked was also high.

The factory manager attended a course on improving the content of work and, when he returned, decided to try out some of the things he had learned. He selected two workers and made each responsible for all the assembly operations — each turning out complete fan assemblies. He also made them inspect their own work and sign the guarantee label which was attached to the fan.

After a brief learning period they began to compete with each other and to take a pride in the quality of the work they turned out. The daily productivity figures changed dramatically.

| OLD SYSTEM | Output 60 | Rejects 10 | % 16 | Net Output 50 | Manhours 24 | Productivity **2,1** per manhour |
|---|---|---|---|---|---|---|
| NEW SYSTEM | 48 | 3 | 6 | 45 | 16 | **2,8** per manhour |

So by decreasing the manpower by 33% and decreasing output by only 10% productivity increased by 33%. A similar decrease resulted in the cost of labour and materials per item thus making the product more profitable and/or more competitive.

The spare worker could either be used full-time or part-time to increase production (if the lower price increased demand) or could be employed in some other productive capacity.

Under today's conditions, no business can afford to ignore the constant need to improve productivity nor can any employee evade his/her responsibility for playing their part in the work of productivity improvement.

And it's not difficult to do once you know the basics involved in measurement, standard setting and method improvement. The two most difficult parts of the operation are, firstly, starting it and secondly, keeping it going. We'll start to tackle the first one in our next chapter.

**Things to Remember**

● Productivity improvement is not a job for specialists only — it should be a part of every job in the organisation.

● Although related, productivity and production are not the same thing. Production is the process of converting resources into products and is measured as the quantity produced in a given time. Productivity is the ratio between the output of a process and its inputs and is measured as output divided by input.

● Productivity improvement requires the optimal use of all resources — manpower, machinery, materials and money — not simply manpower alone.

7

# How productivity is measured

**2**

One of the fundamental principles of productivity improvement is that the productivity of the existing process should be measured in as much detail as possible before any attempt to improve it is made.

At first sight this may appear to be an unnecessary restriction which cuts across many traditional ways of improving productivity, such as employee suggestion plans, think-tanks and the manager's or supervisor's own initiative in changing methods. Almost anyone who is observant can visit an operation and pick up a number of things that could be improved — people standing around, machines idle and so on.

All of these efforts may improve productivity of a particular operation or resource but these may not be the areas where the greatest improvement is needed and can be made. We saw an example of this in the last chapter when the manager picked on manpower for improvement when materials and machinery would both have contributed a greater improvement with less effort.

Alternatively, random efforts to improve may adversely affect the productivity of other resources leaving the company no better off than it was before.

> A purchasing manager found a new material which, being easier to work, substantially reduced the manhours in a process. The works manager was delighted with the change because it improved his labour productivity, which management had been pressuring him to increase.
>
> However, the new material cost more than the old so that the decrease in labour costs was offset by the increase in material costs. Whilst the purchasing manager had used his initiative to improve productivity, in fact the gain had been passed directly to the supplier of the new material and the company had not benefited from it at all.

The only sure way to prevent this happening is to establish accurate measurements of existing productivity so that possible changes can be fully evaluated against them before being introduced.

**Single Resource Productivity**

The first basic measurement is Single Resource Productivity (SRP) which measures the productivity ratio of each individual resource broken down into as much detail as possible.

To obtain Single Resource Productivity the output of a process (in either units or value) is divided by each resource input. The result is then expressed as a productivity ratio.

9

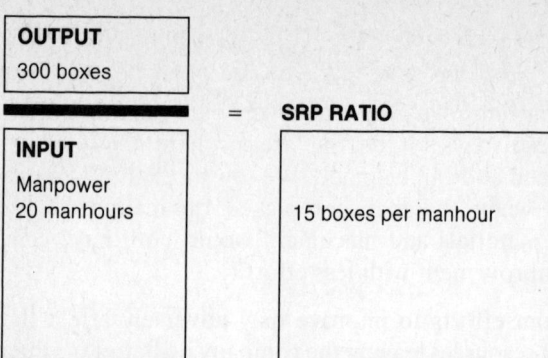

The same method is used to measure all the other inputs of resources into the process.

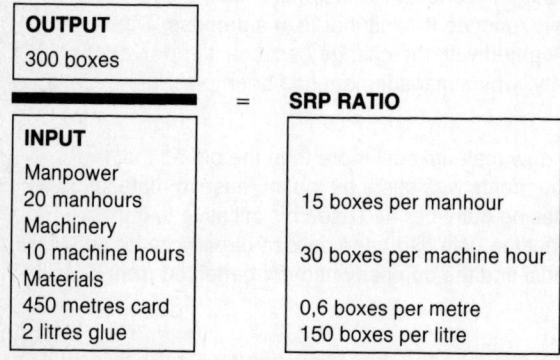

But we said that we should break the various resources into as much detail as possible. For example, what types of labour are employed?

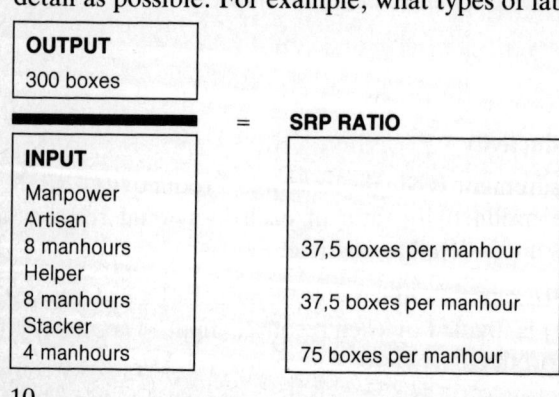

But what about the "stacker" who only does half a job anyway? He collects the finished boxes and places them on a pallet for periodic removal by a forklift truck. He serves two work stations so his time is split between them. Suppose it were possible to rearrange the work station so that, as the helper took a finished box off the machine, he was able to stack it on a suitably placed pallet. The stacker would no longer be required.

The productivity of the artisan and helper would not change but the overall productivity of manpower would increase.

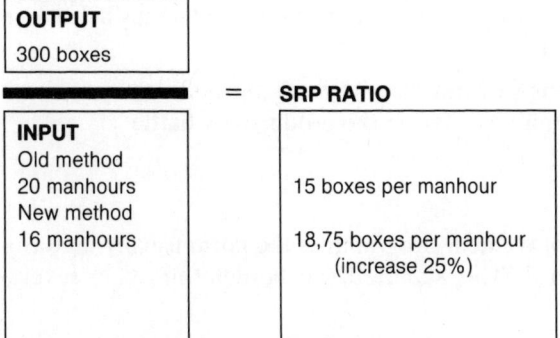

So it is only by measuring Single Resource Productivity in as much detail as possible that you can begin to see where productivity can be improved. Careful measurement also protects you from allowing productivity results to be masked by other factors such as profitability.

The company Chairman concluded his report by saying, "This has been a very difficult year for your company. Like many other employers we have had to meet demands for substantial wage increases and reduced working hours from our workforce. Due to the increase in transport charges our raw material costs have also risen. However, because of the recession in the building industry, our efforts to increase sales volumes have been restricted and they ended up somewhat lower than last year. Luckily we were able to negotiate compensating increases in our selling prices.

As a result I am glad to be able to report that our profits this year are on a par with those of last year and dividends will not be affected. I would like to extend the usual vote of thanks to our Managing Director and his able staff for maintaining the company's productivity during this difficult period."

The Chairman is not unique in confusing profitability and productivity. Profit can always be enhanced by improving productivity but it can also be increased by raising selling prices. In fact, increased selling prices often mask the results of decreased productivity as is obviously the case here. Without SRP ratios to guide you it is not possible to say whether productivity has been gained or lost.

However the SRP ratios alone will not help you much unless you have something to measure them against. Although, in the previous example, an increase of 25% in manpower productivity looks good on paper, 18,75 boxes per manhour may still be less than they achieve in the factory across the street.

Only by comparing your results with a reliable norm can you check whether you are winning or losing the productivity battle.

### Standards

In productivity improvement programmes the norm usually used is a productivity standard. This standard can be determined in several ways.

**Setting productivity standards**

- Use the results of a previous period — last month, last year, etc.
- Use an outstanding result from a previous period.
- Use an industry standard — most industries have developed production norms which they use for planning purposes.
- Establish a required result by work sampling or time study.

The standard gives you something to aim for and something to measure against but it is not static. In fact, it must be changed whenever you change the inputs or the process otherwise its power to motivate will be lost and the results it throws out will be meaningless.

### Productivity Index

Normal company reporting systems are a mixture of positive and negative figures; some indicate good results, some bad. For example when costs go down, that's good but if production goes down, that's bad. Interpreting positive and negative variances in such reports is tricky and time-consuming. Most managers don't even attempt it, relying on their accountants to tell them when things have gone wrong — by which time, of course, it's too late to do much about it.

Since measuring productivity would be a waste of time and effort unless results were constantly reviewed and correctly interpreted, productivity results are always expressed as a percentage of a standard — results above 100% are positive and results below clearly negative. This measure is known as the Productivity Index (PI).

### Productivity Index

$$\frac{\text{Result being measured (actual)} \times 100}{\text{Standard}} = \text{P.I.}$$

The result being measured is multiplied by 100 so that the PI will be expressed as a percentage of the standard (100). Let's see how it works in practice. First you must find the Single Resource Productivity ratios of the process — in this case a gang making concrete with a small mixer.

**OUTPUT 24** cubic metres (m³) of concrete

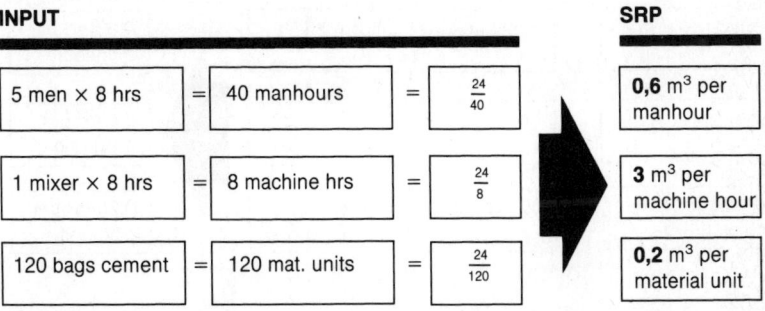

| INPUT | | | SRP |
|---|---|---|---|
| 5 men × 8 hrs | = 40 manhours | = $\frac{24}{40}$ | **0,6** m³ per manhour |
| 1 mixer × 8 hrs | = 8 machine hrs | = $\frac{24}{8}$ | **3** m³ per machine hour |
| 120 bags cement | = 120 mat. units | = $\frac{24}{120}$ | **0,2** m³ per material unit |

At this stage you don't know whether these results are good or bad until you can compare them with some standard, in this case an industry norm, and calculate Productivity Indices for each ratio.

| Input | SRP | Standard | | PI |
|---|---|---|---|---|
| Manpower | 0,6 | 0,75 | $\dfrac{0,6 \times 100}{0,75}$ = | 80% |
| Machinery | 3,0 | 3,0 | $\dfrac{3,0 \times 100}{3,0}$ = | 100% |
| Material | 0,2 | 0,25 | $\dfrac{0,2 \times 100}{0,25}$ = | 80% |

Now you can see at a glance that you are running 20% below standard in manpower and materials. In each case you are getting less output from your resources than you should and therefore the finished product is costing more than it should. Obviously something must be done.

So you ask the foreman to reduce his gang by two men and to give them a proper measure for the cement so that they can only mix the correct amount. What happens to the SRP?

**OUTPUT 24** cubic metres (m³) of concrete
**INPUT**                                                              **SRP**

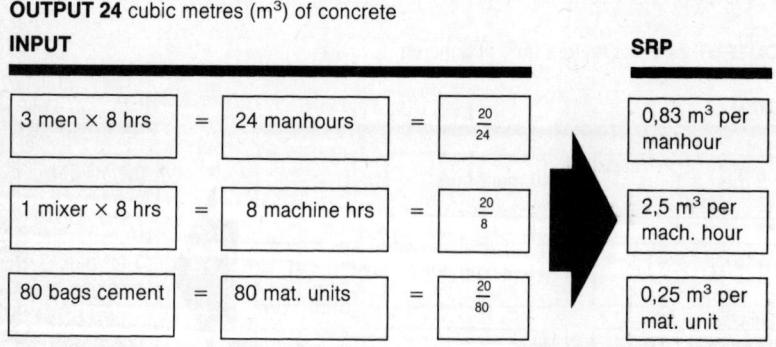

| 3 men × 8 hrs | = | 24 manhours | = | $\frac{20}{24}$ | | 0,83 m³ per manhour |
| 1 mixer × 8 hrs | = | 8 machine hrs | = | $\frac{20}{8}$ | | 2,5 m³ per mach. hour |
| 80 bags cement | = | 80 mat. units | = | $\frac{20}{80}$ | | 0,25 m³ per mat. unit |

The smaller gang wasn't able to keep up the same rate of production as the larger gang but productivity of manpower and materials seems to have improved. Let's check the Productivity Indices of the new method.

14

| Input | SRP | Standard | | | PI |
|---|---|---|---|---|---|
| Manpower | 0,83 | 0,75 | $\dfrac{0,83 \times 100}{0,75}$ | = | 111% |
| Machinery | 2,5 | 3,0 | $\dfrac{2,5 \times 100}{3,0}$ | = | 83% |
| Materials | 0,25 | 0,25 | $\dfrac{0,25 \times 100}{0,25}$ | = | 100% |

Apart from the fact that overall production is down (which may or may not be critical depending on the production plan) the foreman seems to have got well above the standard productivity from his gang and to have corrected the cement problem. But he dropped back 17% on machine productivity. Has the overall result been positive or negative? To find this out you need to use the second basic measure of productivity.

**Total Resource Productivity**

So far we have been concentrating on the productivity of the individual inputs into a process, and we have seen how changes in input and output can affect productivity. However, sometimes an improvement in the productivity of one resource input will cause a deterioration in another (as in the last example). In these cases you need to be able to check and compare the overall productivity of the process. For this purpose we use Total Resource Productivity (TRP).

In order to find the TRP all inputs are converted into monetary values, added together and divided into the output to establish the output per Rand of input. Let's apply it first to the old method of making concrete.

**OLD METHOD**

**INPUT**

| | | | **OUTPUT** |
|---|---|---|---|
| 40 manhours @ R1,5 | R 60 | | **24** m³ |
| 8 mach. hours @ R15 | R120 | **R900** | concrete |
| 120 mat. units @ R6 | R720 | | |

TOTAL RESOURCE
PRODUCTIVITY $= \dfrac{24}{900} =$ **0,026** m³ per Rand of input

15

Using the same input values you can calculate the TRP of the new method.

**NEW METHOD**

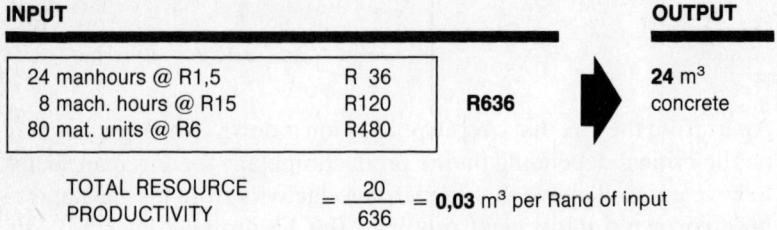

**INPUT**                                      **OUTPUT**

| | | | |
|---|---|---|---|
| 24 manhours @ R1,5 | R 36 | | **24** m$^3$ |
| 8 mach. hours @ R15 | R120 | **R636** | concrete |
| 80 mat. units @ R6 | R480 | | |

$$\text{TOTAL RESOURCE PRODUCTIVITY} = \frac{20}{636} = \textbf{0,03} \text{ m}^3 \text{ per Rand of input}$$

Checking the Productivity Indices of old and new methods you can see whether or not the changes made by the foreman have in fact increased overall productivity.

$$PI = \frac{\text{actual} \times 100}{\text{standard}} = \frac{0,03 \times 100}{0,026} = \textbf{115\%}$$

So you have improved by 15% which seems very good but is it the best you can get? Using the previous standards as a guide the standard TRP for the process works out at 0,032 m$^3$ per Rand input. You can now measure your new performance against the standard.

$$PI = \frac{\text{actual} \times 100}{\text{standard}} = \frac{0,03 \times 100}{0,032} = \textbf{94\%}$$

So, although you have done well to improve productivity you still need to improve some more which will probably mean bringing back another man to get the production up and keep the machine operating at 100% capacity. And of course you don't have to be satisfied with reaching the standard — you can always try to beat it.

One last point — always use the same base costs when calculating the Total Resource Productivity of more than one process or the same process at different times (eg last year versus this year). Obviously changes in costs will throw out the validity of the comparison.

**Things to Remember**

● Single Resource Productivity measures the productivity of each individual input as a ratio of output to input. The more detailed the breakdown of inputs the greater your ability to spot areas needing action.

● Standards of productivity must be set so that results can be compared with a standard to provide meaningful variances for investigation.

● Productivity Index is a method of uniformly reporting results as a percentage of standard performance.

● Total Resource Productivity is used to compare the overall productivity of all resource inputs with other results or standards. It is found by converting all the inputs into monetary values, adding them together and dividing them into the output to give the output per Rand of total input.

● It is a fundamental principle of productivity improvement that productivity should be measured before any attempt is made to improve it. Equally important is to ensure it is remeasured after every change in the process or resource inputs.

● Reporting productivity results as indices of standards should form a part of the regular reporting system of any company that seriously wants to improve its productivity.

# What influences productivity?

**3**

We have already demonstrated how productivity can be affected by changing inputs. This is only one of the factors which can affect productivity. There are many others which can be broadly classified under the headings of physical and psychological influences.

By physical influences we mean the tangible factors involved in the process which can affect productivity. By psychological factors we refer to the behavioural patterns of management and employees which can often have equally powerful effects on productivity. Let's look at the physical influences first.

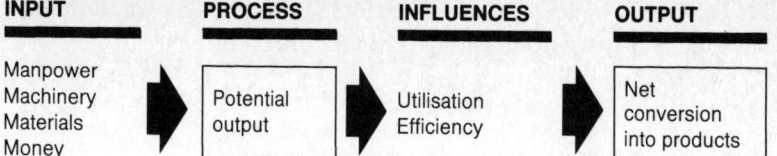

| INPUT | PROCESS | INFLUENCES | OUTPUT |
|-------|---------|------------|--------|
| Manpower Machinery Materials Money | Potential output | Utilisation Efficiency | Net conversion into products |

The many physical influences restricting the potential output, and thus the productivity of a process, can be grouped under two factors — utilisation and efficiency. Utilisation refers to the degree to which the resources committed to a process are actually converted into the product, whilst efficiency concerns the speed and accuracy with which the conversion is accomplished.

### Utilisation

Dealing firstly with utilisation we can best demonstrate its effect on the *manpower* resource with this diagram.

| TOTAL MANHOURS AVAILABLE | | | |
|---|---|---|---|
| **IDLE** | | **WORK** | |
| LOST TIME | | EXTRA WORK | PRODUCTIVE WORK |
| WORKER | MANAGEMENT | EXTRA WORK | PRODUCTIVE WORK |
| **UNPRODUCTIVE** | | **PRODUCTIVE** | |

The total manhours available are the hours in the official working day (or week or month) for which the employee is paid and which vary from industry to industry. This total period can be broken down into time spent *idle* and time spent at *work*.

Idle time is made up of time lost by the *workers* themselves or by *management* inefficiencies. Here are some of the causes.

**Time lost by workers**
- Absenteeism
- Tardiness
- Exceeding agreed rest periods
- Unnecessary stoppages

**Time lost by management inefficiencies**
- Poor work planning
- Delays in material supply
- Poor working conditions
- Unnecessary down-time

19

*Extra work* is the unnecessary work done by the worker when actually working and can be caused by a number of conditions.

**Causes of extra work**
- Inefficient work methods (lack of training)
- Badly designed layout of the job
- Incorrect or poorly adjusted tools
- Difficult work process
- Re-working rejects

The balance of the available time is used for *productive work*. Although the diagram on the previous page may seem to be drawn out of proportion it is unfortunately true that, in many operations which have not studied productivity improvement, effective manpower utilisation seldom exceeds 50 percent.

A large refinery always employed outside contractors to carry out its annual shut-down overhaul. The work was put out to tender, the contractor tendering to complete the work in accordance with plans and detailed specifications supplied by the engineering department of the refinery who maintained a controlling function on the contract. Casual observation by the supervising engineers indicated that a lot of time was being wasted by the artisan and unskilled staff employed by the contractor. Since this would affect the productivity of manpower and hence the costs of the contractor, they decided to monitor the situation carefully the following year.

Accordingly they employed a consultant to measure the utilisation of the labour force employed by the contractor. At the end of his study he produced the following summary of his findings:

**Time lost due to management inefficiencies**

| | |
|---|---|
| Poor planning | 8,1 |
| Materials delays | 2,7 |
| Maintenance | 3,1 |
| Sub-total | 13,9 |

**Time lost by workers**

| | |
|---|---|
| Idle | 34,7 |

**Extra work**

| | |
|---|---|
| Unnecessary walking | 5,6 |

*Total unproductive time* **54,2%**    *Productive time* **45,8%**

Using these figures they suggested to the contractors that they improve their management and supervision in future contracts and were able to negotiate a keener price the following year as a result. This is yet another example of the real money value of measuring productivity.

The utilisation of *machinery* follows a similar pattern to that of manpower, being closely linked to the behaviour of its operators.

**TOTAL MACHINE HOURS AVAILABLE**

| IDLE | | OPERATING | |
|---|---|---|---|
| LOST CAPACITY | | REJECTS | PRODUCTS |
| OPERATOR | MANAGEMENT | | |
| UNPRODUCTIVE | | | PRODUCTIVE |

Strictly speaking the machine should be available for 24 hours per day less time needed for routine maintenance. However, machine utilisation is normally measured against the working day of the operation (ie one, two or three shifts).

The causes of *lost capacity* are essentially the same as for manpower utilisation, ie split between worker and management, but usually with more emphasis on poor work planning or scheduling and excessive down-time.

*Rejects* represent an unproductive use of all the resources, and therefore an unnecessary increase in costs, which should be avoided. The call today is for "Zero defects" or "Get it right first time" and certainly many successful companies make it their policy. However there is another school of thought which believes it is more costly to ensure perfection than it is to correct a few errors and that a strictly controlled percentage of rejects is therefore acceptable. Perhaps in the end it will be the increasingly discerning consumer who will dictate the policy.

**Causes of rejects**

● Machines badly maintained and set
● Machines incorrectly operated
● Defective material used
● Quality standard set too high.

Machines can vary in cost from less than R100 to several millions and their standing costs (ie cost of capital or lease, space, operators) can vary in proportion. As these costs increase the need to maximise utilisation becomes paramount.

A packaging company operated two large bag-forming machines. These machines took in rolls of paper which they then cut, folded, printed and glued, finally producing completed bags at the rate of 8–10 000 per hour. The machines had to be shut down periodically for cleaning up the surplus glue and ink which accumulated and soiled the finished bags causing them to be rejected. Whenever the type of bag or printing required had to be changed, the machines were shut down whilst a fitter and his mate carried out the necessary changes. This process took about 5 hours plus another hour during which minor running adjustments had to be made. During this latter period the reject rate was high.

The machines, which cost about 1,25 million rands each when purchased some years ago, were designed to handle long runs of the same product and performed exceptionally well on this type of work. However, in recent years, as the price of the product increased, customers reduced their stocks and started to order on a hand to mouth basis. Changeovers became more frequent and down-time increased.

One day a visitor from Head Office happened to visit the plant when both machines were being changed and their operators standing idle. He asked the factory manager what the percentage down-time was on the machines. The factory manager, who hadn't checked on his productivity for some time, because he thought it was a lot of nonsense, sent for the records and was horrified to see that down-time had reached 46% of available time.

He immediately blamed the sales department for the small orders they were asking him to make up. His visitor pointed out that, at the moment, the down-time was costing the company in the region of R2 000 per hour for loss of output, to say nothing of labour and standing costs of nearly R100 per hour. Multiply that by 46% of a 16-hour day and downtime was costing over R15 000 per day.

The visitor added that, at that rate, there was a great deal that could be done to improve utilisation and productivity — such as making for stock, increasing the size of the changeover teams, modifying the cleaning procedures and so on — which could result in the down-time being brought down to an acceptable level.

The factory manager now checks the utilisation of all his machines daily and will never forget his lesson that it is no good keeping productivity records unless you monitor them constantly and take action to correct the problems they show up.

Because of its high contribution to total costs in most manufacturing processes the utilisation of *material* plays a major role in productivity. The pattern is similar to that for manpower and machinery.

### TOTAL MATERIAL PURCHASED

| NOT PROCESSED | | PROCESSED | |
|---|---|---|---|
| WASTED | | SPOILT | PRODUCTS |
| WORKER | MANAGEMENT | | |
| UNPRODUCTIVE | | | PRODUCTIVE |

Out of the total material purchased a proportion does not reach the process at all, being *wasted* either by the actions of *workers* or by the inefficiencies of *management*.

**Causes of wastage**

*Worker*

- Spillage
- Damage in handling
- Shrinkage (theft)
- Waste

*Management*

- Bad storage conditions
- Poor quality material
- Incorrect material
- Product design

Often material is *spoilt* in the actual process as we saw in the case of the bags which were soiled by glue and ink. There are many causes of spoilage in a process. Here are some of them.

**Causes of spoilt material**

- Machine wrongly set
- Contamination
- Incorrect application
- Untrained operators
- Difficult operation
- Poor design of process

Utilisation measures what you productively use out of the resources you put into a process (industry or service). The better your utilisation the better your productivity and vice versa. If you haven't measured the utilisation of your resources it would certainly pay you to do so — you might be in for a shock.

A few weeks ago I had breakfast in a country hotel. The waiter came from the kitchen to show me to a table and then returned to fetch a menu. He took my order and disappeared into the kitchen. After a short time he brought me orange juice, returning to the kitchen. In due course he returned with toast and butter, and then, after a short delay, brought eggs and bacon. I asked him to bring the coffee I had ordered, which he did. When I had finished the eggs, I asked him for marmalade for which he returned to the kitchen. Finally, I asked for the bill which he brought from the same source to which he took my credit card, eventually returning it with the docket for my signature.

Before I left I paced out the distance from my table to the kitchen. It was about 12 metres and he had made a total of 15 trips, walking nearly 200 metres in the process. He richly deserved the tip I left him!

I subsequently read that waitresses in fast-food restaurants in the USA regularly "cover" up to 10 tables each whilst in this country 4 to 5 is the maximum. I'm not surprised.

Measuring utilisation will tell you to what degree your resources are being productively employed but it won't tell you how well they are being used. To learn this you need to measure efficiency.

**Efficiency**

Efficiency, as we have said, is the measure of the speed and accuracy with which work is completed. Speed is obviously important because the faster the piece of work can be completed the greater the productivity of manpower and machinery. However, if the work is not done accurately it will be rejected and productivity will suffer. It is therefore necessary to maintain a balance between speed and accuracy.

The speed with which work is completed can be measured roughly by "work sampling" or, more accurately, by "time study", both of which will be explained in the next chapter.

The accuracy of a process is measured by "quality control" which involves checking the products against pre-set criteria, either individually or by sampling. The quality of a service operation can be similarly checked by inspecting the ongoing operation or by polling customers — hence the many questionnaires you are asked to fill in by hotels, airlines and garages, etc.

The physical factors affecting efficiency also stem from both worker and management action or omission.

#### Factors affecting efficiency

- Workers' aptitude and skill (training)
- Layout of the work (eliminating wasted effort)
- Simplicity of the work method
- Provision of correct tools and aids
- Working conditions (atmosphere, light, noise, etc.)

Failure by management to provide for any of these factors will have an adverse effect on efficiency and, hence, on productivity. However, it is possible to provide all the above and still not reach the required standards of efficiency. The reason lies in the second series of factors influencing productivity, namely the psychological influences.

## Phychological Influences

The psychological influences are the things which affect the behaviour of the worker and determine whether he will be a dedicated achiever or a confirmed loafer and fall roughly into two classifications:

## Demotivators

Demotivators are the conditions in the work environment which tend to frustrate the worker and create conditions which are not conducive to whole-hearted effort on his part.

#### Demotivators

- Unnecessary restrictions, procedures and red-tape.
- Untrained or inexperienced supervisors.
- Poor inter-personal relationships with supervisor/colleagues.
- Sub-standard remuneration.
- Absence of agreed grievance and disciplinary procedures.

The ultimate measure of demotivation is when workers go slow or eventually strike. An analysis of strike patterns over the last few years seems to indicate that, eliminating obviously political or ideological causes, a majority of the remaining problems stem from one or all of the demotivators listed above.

It is important to remember that the demotivators are based on the perceptions of the worker — not of management. Management may consider it perfectly justifiable to expect the worker to change into his work clothes in his own time whereas the worker may perceive it as an unnecessary restriction. How many managements ever ask the workers to appraise their supervisors? Or check the relationship in the work group? And yet inefficient supervisors cause many thousands of lost manhours of productivity, all too often without the knowledge of management.

We have dealt here with the demotivators over which management has direct control. There are other, off-the-job factors which sometimes have a greater influence on motivation and productivity.

Jonas Mdlala stretched out to quieten the alarm clock which was threatening to jump off the box beside the camp bed. It was four-thirty and as cold as the welcome he got from the timekeeper yesterday when he was late clocking in.

He felt as if he had hardly slept at all. It was nearly eight last night before he got home. He'd had to work overtime because some fool had broken the line-feeder in the middle of making up a rush order and it wasn't repaired until four o'clock. By the time he'd had a drink at Polly's place and had something to eat it was nearly ten.

He lit the candle stub and tried to find his trousers in the crowded room. They were on the floor where he had dropped them. Going outside into the frost-covered yard he drew water and washed briefly. There was no time for food — nor any if he had wanted it.

By five o'clock he left the shack and became one of the unrecognisable, hunched figures shuffling towards the bus stop. There was already a queue and he had to wait for the next bus. It was still dark when he reached the station and fought his way over the bridge to the platform.

The train was already quite full and he had to stand. By the time he got to the city it was six-thirty and he joined the group of workers walking towards the factory. A big man caught his arm and said he had watched him working on the rush order yesterday. He was working too quickly. If the study man saw him he would change the rate for the job and a lot of people would lose their jobs. Jonas wouldn't want that to happen, would he, he said, giving his arm a brutal twist.

By seven, when it was just getting light, Jonas had clocked in, changed into his coveralls and taken his place at his work station. When the buzzer went he yawned and started another dreary day.

## Motivators

The motivators are the conditions management can create to help each worker obtain satisfaction from his work and produce of his best.

### motivators

- Participation in decisions which affect them.
- Responsibility within defined limits.
- Feedback of results and recognition for good work.
- Interesting work — multiple tasks and self-control.
- Monetary rewards in line with achievement.

There's nothing startlingly new about those five points — they've been around a long time and what they really boil down to is simply treating people like people and not as disposable chattels. What is startling is that so few companies practice them when they can have such a marked effect on productivity.

Standard time study procedures show that the difference between the output of an unmotivated worker as opposed to a motivated one can be as much as 60%. The only cost involved in making this improvement is a little managerial time and effort.

## Things to Remember

- Productivity can be influenced by both physical and psychological factors. The most important physical influences are utilisation and efficiency.

- Utilisation is the degree to which resources are converted into product whilst efficiency measures the speed and accuracy with which they are converted.

- Manpower and machinery utilisation is reduced by the time lost by the workers or operators and by management inefficiencies. Manpower utilisation is further reduced by the extra, unnecessary work done. Similarly, machine utilisation is further reduced by the rejects produced which have to be scrapped or re-worked.

- Material utilisation is reduced by what is wasted before getting into the process either by the users or by management inefficiencies. It is further reduced by material spoilt in the actual process and scrapped.

- Both the speed and accuracy with which work is done can be accurately measured to establish the efficiency of a worker and any physical barriers to standard output can be corrected.

- Although the physical conditions of the work environment may be ideal, psychological influences may still prevent the worker achieving standard output. These influences may be expressed as motivators and demotivators.

- Demotivators are the conditions in the work environment which frustrate the worker whilst motivators are conditions which help the worker obtain satisfaction from the work and so help to increase his/her output.

- Eliminating demotivators and optimising motivators is the cheapest and quickest way to improve the productivity of any operation.

# How to measure utilisation and efficiency

So far we have been talking about how valuable it is to measure productivity but we haven't said much about how it can be measured. Let's rectify that now.

Most manufacturing operations employ specialists to measure productivity and set work standards. Larger service operators bring in consultants to help them when necessary. Thus managers generally regard the measurement process as being a complication which is not part of their job.

This is a pity, because there is nothing to touch it as a means of really seeing what is happening in the workplace, which is so necessary for

29

innovative management. Hence the recent stress laid on "managing by walking around" if you are searching for excellent performance.

We don't expect to see C.E.O.'s clutching stopwatches but there is no reason why supervisors and junior managers can't become involved. It is really quite simple and can be done during the normal working routine. There are three basic techniques involved, Activity Sampling, Work Sampling and Time Study. The first measures utilisation and the last two efficiency. Here's how they work.

## Activity Sampling

If you want to find out how much of their time workers are spending on the productive activities which make up their jobs and how much on other non-productive activities, the most accurate way is to watch an individual for a full day several times in a month and then average the results.

However, this is not only time consuming for you, it is also most disturbing for the worker who will probably not behave normally when watched. Activity Sampling is a method which will overcome both of these problems provided you can accept slightly less than a guaranteed 100% accuracy.

In our last chapter we talked about sampling in terms of quality control. Instead of subjecting every item produced to a test, samples are taken at intervals for testing and the results applied statistically to the whole production run. If 5% of the samples fail to pass the tests then it is assumed that the reject rate for the whole run will be about the same.

The same principle can be applied to work. First of all the work can be broken down into its component activities or "elements" as they are called. Then, at pre-determined intervals, the worker can be observed and the precise element being performed recorded. In its simplest form, the elements of a job can be described as "work" and "no work" and can be measured like this.

**22 observations**

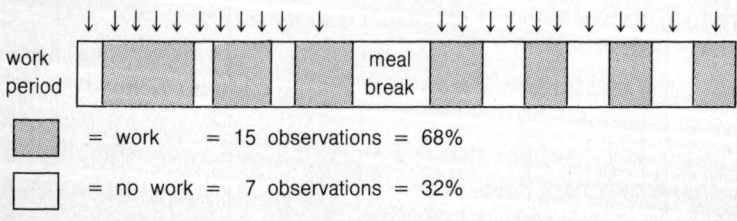

| | = work | = 15 observations | = 68% |
| | = no work | = 7 observations | = 32% |

Taking 22 observations of a worker during the day, it appears that 15 of them or 68% occurred when work was being done and 7 or 32% when no work was being done. If you were to measure the shaded and unshaded areas of the diagram you would find that this is approximately the actual division between them.

Note we say "approximately" because a sample can never give absolute accuracy. Obviously the more samples taken, the more accurate the results are likely to be. Also, the greater the proportion of time taken up by an element the lower the number of samples required to get a reasonably accurate result. Conversely, the smaller it is the more samples you will have to take to be sure of "catching" it in your sample net.

If you want to be precise you can calculate the number of observations needed to give you a reasonable accuracy (95%) with formula "A". Alternatively you can use formula "B" to tell you how accurate your result will be for any given number of observations.

**A.** Number of observations for 5% deviation

$$N = \frac{4p(100 - p)}{L^2}$$

**B.** Accuracy of a number of observations

$$L = 2\sqrt{\frac{p(100 - p)}{N}}$$

N = number of observations
p = approximate time of element studied
L = accuracy as a percentage

In the detailed study of an oil refinery we quoted in the previous chapter the consultant had to make several hundred observations because the elements were each a small part of the total. However, if you wanted to check out a normal service or production operation (such as labourers digging a ditch) 50-100 observations would be sufficient to give you a reasonable result.

Although making 100 observations may sound like a lot of extra work for a supervisor or junior manager it can be done very easily if combined with routine visits to the work site. For example, simply walking through an office, store or factory area five times a day will provide 25 observations a week and 100 in a month. Preferably the visits should be made at different times each day if you want to cover the normal working pattern.

Following a course in productivity awareness, the supervisor of a warehouse decided to take an activity sample of the work done by his two forklift trucks. He decided to take 100 samples by observing what they were doing every time he walked through the warehouse, which was usually several times a day. The elements he wanted to check were travelling, stacking, loading (standing with a pallet while it was being loaded with cartons), idle and maintenance. At the end of a month he had these results:

| | Machine 1 | Machine 2 | Using 1 truck |
|---|---|---|---|
| Travelling | 32 | 30 | 62 |
| Stacking | 15 | 12 | 27 |
| Loading | (20) | (18) | |
| Idle | 25 | 29 | 11 |
| Maintenance | (8) | (11) | |
| | 100 | 100 | 100 |

He saw from the figures that if he could eliminate the wasteful practice of having the forklift stand while a pallet was loaded, and arrange for the maintenance to be done outside normal hours, he could get by with only one forklift truck and still allow the operator sufficient time to rest. This would double the productivity of his machine resource and reduce his costs considerably, even allowing for maintenance being done out of normal working hours.

Doing the study didn't add to his workload but it did bring home to him how productive time was being lost through poor work planning and enabled him to manage his operation more efficiently.

Before starting a study like this you have to do two things — decide what elements you want to check, and draw up a form to record your observations. When deciding what elements to check remember that they must be visually distinct, ie you must be able to identify them at a glance (it would be difficult to identify an employee thinking!). The form should be kept as simple as possible.

You can record the observations by making a tick (✔) against the observed element or by using strokes and cancelling every fifth one (卌) as we have done in the example — it makes it easier to count in fives.

32

| Element | Machine 1 Observation | | Machine 2 Observation | |
|---|---|---|---|---|
| Travelling | ⊦⊦⊦ ⊦⊦⊦ // ⊦⊦⊦ ⊦⊦⊦ ⊦⊦⊦ ⊦⊦⊦ | 32 | ⊦⊦⊦ ⊦⊦⊦ ⊦⊦⊦ ⊦⊦⊦ ⊦⊦⊦ ⊦⊦⊦ | 30 |
| Stacking | ⊦⊦⊦ ⊦⊦⊦ ⊦⊦⊦ | 15 | ⊦⊦⊦ ⊦⊦⊦ // | 12 |
| Loading | ⊦⊦⊦ ⊦⊦⊦ ⊦⊦⊦ ⊦⊦⊦ | 20 | ⊦⊦⊦ ⊦⊦⊦ ⊦⊦⊦ /// | 18 |
| Idle | ⊦⊦⊦ ⊦⊦⊦ ⊦⊦⊦ ⊦⊦⊦ ⊦⊦⊦ | 25 | ⊦⊦⊦ ⊦⊦⊦ ⊦⊦⊦ ⊦⊦⊦ ⊦⊦⊦ ⊦⊦⊦ | 29 |
| Maintenance | ⊦⊦⊦ /// | 8 | ⊦⊦⊦ ⊦⊦⊦ / | 11 |
| | TOTAL | 100 | TOTAL | 100 |

Activity Sampling, then, gives you a relatively easy way to check the utilisation of manpower and machinery, and provides an excellent base from which to move into productivity improvement studies.

However, we have agreed on the necessity for measuring existing productivity before we select areas for improvement and this means we need standards to measure against. Two of the methods of setting standards that we mentioned in Chapter 2 were Work Sampling and Time Study.

## Work Sampling

If you want to find out how long it takes to complete a piece of work you can do so quite easily by recording how much has been done during the time you sample activities.

| | | | |
|---|---|---|---|
| Time of first observation | 0910 | Pallets stacked | 2 |
| Time of last observation | 1122 | Pallets stacked | 35 |
| Time elapsed | 132 mins. | Pallets stacked | 33 |

$$\text{Time per pallet} \quad \frac{132}{33} = 4 \text{ minutes}$$

This is the total time spent per pallet and includes all the unproductive time you recorded in your activity sampling. Therefore to find the correct time it should take per pallet, you must eliminate the unproductive time.

33

| Observed time per pallet | 4 mins. |
|---|---|
| Observed unproductive time = 55% = 2,2 mins. | |
| Correct time per pallet | 1,8 mins. |

You can use this result to set a standard for the productivity of the forklift trucks and can measure the present operation against the standard to find the present Productivity Index.

Pallets per machine hour (observed) $\dfrac{60}{4} = 15$

Pallets per machine hour (standard) $\dfrac{60}{1,8} = 33$

$$P.I. = \frac{R2 \times 100}{R1} = \frac{15 \times 100}{33} = 45\%$$

So Work Sampling is a very quick and simple method of arriving at a standard for measuring productivity. However, it doesn't take into account the efficiency of the operator — it is based on *what is done* rather than on what *should be done*. If you need a more accurate standard you will have carry out a Time Study.

**Time Study**

The purpose of time study is to establish a standard time for a piece of work — "standard time" being the time it should take an average, motivated worker (taking adequate care and without undue stress or fatigue) to complete the work. It represents a pace of working which can be maintained all day and should be a fair assessment of what can be expected from a worker given the type of job and the environment in which it is performed.

Standard time is a fundamental input to both production planning and productivity measurement. It is commonly employed in manufacturing operations but is less common (although equally necessary) in service operations. As we have said, time study is usually carried out by specialist personnel; however, any manager with some time at his disposal can apply the technique. In any event he should understand how it is done and thus be able to accept (or reject if necessary) the standards to which his employees are asked to work.

As in activity sampling, the first step in time study is to break the job down into visually distinct elements. This is usually done by observing the job through several cycles before starting the study. Next you need to obtain a stopwatch (preferably a digital one that measures in decimals of a minute because decimals are easier to add and subtract than seconds) and to design a form. Here is a simple one:

| ELEMENT NO | DESCRIPTION | WATCH READING | OBSERVED TIME | RATING | BASIC TIME |
|---|---|---|---|---|---|
| | | | | | |

These are only the headings — the form would probably extend downwards for 30 or so lines. The first step is to enter the elements in order, describing each one and then numbering them.

As soon as you are ready to start timing you wait for the beginning of the first element and start the watch running, leaving it running until you have completed your study. As soon as the first element has been completed you record the time and continue recording the time of completion for each of the elements in the same way.

The time taken for each element is found by subtracting the time of completion of the first element from the time of completion of the next element, and so on through the study. This time is called the "observed time" and is entered in the column provided on your form. You'll find the subtraction much easier if you start at the bottom of the form and work upwards as we have done on the next page.

Adding up the times for all the elements will give you the total for the job. This is the time taken by the person observed. But not all people are equally skilful at pouring beer. Some pour it more slowly, others pour it too quickly and have to wait for the froth to subside. So an individual performance like this is likely to be misleading unless you can relate it to a standard performance.

The standard performance in this case is the efficiency of an average, well-trained and motivated worker working at 100% of his/her ability. Since these are as scarce as hen's teeth in most operations, how do you find such a standard performance?

| Element | Description | Reading | Observed time | Rating | Basic time |
|---|---|---|---|---|---|
| 6 | REPLACE OPENER | 2,91 | 0,12 | | |
| 5 | REPLACE BOTTLE | 2,79 | 0,12 | | |
| 4 | POUR BEER | 2,67 | 2,00 | | |
| 3 | OPEN BOTTLE | 0,67 | 0,17 | | |
| 2 | PICK UP OPENER | 0,50 | 0,25 | | |
| 1 | PICK UP BOTTLE | 0,25 | 0,25 | | |
| | | 0,00 | 2,91 | | |

## Work Rating

The method used to establish standard performance is known as "work rating" and is the assessment of the efficiency (speed and accuracy) with which a worker performs a job, measured on a scale of 0-100. Standard performance is 100 but measurements above can be recorded in exceptional cases.

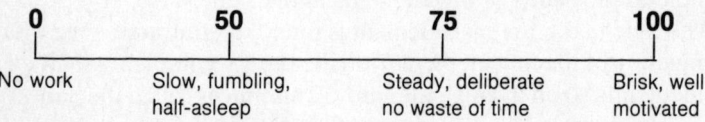

| 0 | 50 | 75 | 100 |
|---|---|---|---|
| No work | Slow, fumbling, half-asleep | Steady, deliberate no waste of time | Brisk, well motivated |

The worker is observed at work and is mentally compared with a visual image of how he would be working at 100% and then "rated" accordingly.

To enable you to visualise "rating" here are some examples —

● a gang of municipal employees digging a trench would probably rate between 50-60 (when working!)

● John McEnroe trying for match point would usually operate at about 125 or more.

● a typist turning out 60 words per minute would be rated at 100 (provided her work was error free).

36

You can practise rating yourself — the waiter at lunch, the
service-station attendant, the airways booking clerk and so on."

Rating is at best a subjective assessment of the worker observed and
therefore skill and practice are necessary if the ratings are to be
consistent. When the standards are to be used for wage rate determina-
tion it is advisable to use trained specialists for rating. Training courses
are available which allow the aspiring rater to experience a vast
number of work situations in a relatively short time and thereby
acquire judgemental ability.

Where the need for absolute accuracy is not so great, particularly in
service industries, it has been our experience that supervisors and
foremen usually have a sound judgemental standard of the work they
supervise and, with a little practice, can produce ratings accurate
enough for setting productivity standards. One of the great advantages
of using their experience in this way is that, having participated in
setting the standard they are likely to ensure that it is achieved.

**Basic Time**

The time you have measured so far is the observed time (OT) — the
actual time taken. The rating (R) you have given the worker tells you
what percentage of standard efficiency is being achieved. In order to
find the time it should take to do the job at standard efficiency you have
to adjust the observed time by this percentage. The resultant time is
known as "basic time".

So, to find basic time you simply multiply observed time by the
rating percentage $(\frac{R}{100})$

$$\text{BASIC TIME} = \frac{\text{OT} \times \text{R}}{100}$$

In the example overleaf we have rated each element but, in practice,
since the total operation is less than 1,5 minutes in duration, you could
rate the total operation and use this average to determine basic times.
We have only shown one cycle of six elements in our example but, in
practice, you would need to take several cycles and average them to
arrive at an accurate basic time for the job. As a rough guide, if the
principal element of the cycle is longer than 1 minute, and the variation
between times is not more than 0,3 minutes, averaging 15 observations
will give you an accurracy within 10%. If your variation is greater than

| Element | Description | Reading | Observed time | Rating | Basic time |
|---|---|---|---|---|---|
| 6 | REPLACE OPENER | 2,91 | 0,12 | 100 | 0,12 |
| 5 | REPLACE BOTTLE | 2,79 | 0,12 | 80 | 0,10 |
| 4 | POUR BEER | 2,67 | 2,00 | 75 | 1,50 |
| 3 | OPEN BOTTLE | 0,67 | 0,17 | 60 | 0,10 |
| 2 | PICK UP OPENER | 0,50 | 0,25 | 80 | 0,20 |
| 1 | PICK UP BOTTLE | 0,25 | 0,25 | 75 | 0,19 |
| | | 0,00 | 2,91 | | 1,76 |

30% you will have to take more times but it will seldom be necessary to take more than 30.

**Relaxation Allowances**

Basic time tells you how long it should take a motivated worker to do the job working without stopping, but not even a highly motivated worker can work all day without rest. So some time has to be allowed for rest and personal needs. This time is calculated at a percentage of basic time and the usual standard allowances are those agreed by the International Labour Office (ILO). Here are some of them:

**REST AND PERSONAL ALLOWANCES**

| | | Men | Women |
|---|---|---|---|
| **A.** Always given | | | |
| Basic allowance | | 9 | 11* |
| **B.** Given where necessary | | | |
| Standing | | 2 | 4* |
| Awkward position | | 2 | 3 |
| Use of force | 2,5 kg | 0 | 1 |
| | 10 kg | 3 | 4 |
| | 20 kg | 10 | 15 |
| Monotony | | 2 | 1* |

So a barmaid, pouring beer, would be allowed 11* + 4* + 1* or 16% of 1,76 minutes which is 0,28 minutes. This added to her basic time of

1,76 would give a total of 2,04 minutes per bottle. At this rate she would be expected to open 29 bottles per hour ($\frac{60}{2,04}$) and be able to chat to you for 10 minutes per hour. This would certainly not be fast enough for the rush hour in a South African pub and you would have to find ways of making the job easier so that she could produce more without expending greater effort or upsetting the customers!

**Process and Special Allowances**

An operator working with a machine will often have to wait for the machine to complete an element before being able to commence the next element of his/her work.

| Operator switches on duplicator | Machine warms up | Operator loads machine | Machine runs off copies | Operator unloads copies |
|---|---|---|---|---|

This enforced idleness is treated as a "process allowance" and the actual time involved in waiting for the machine is added to the basic time. Special allowances cover items which do not occur on each cycle such as start-up, shut-down, clean-up, etc. These are pro-rated across the working day and added as a percentage to basic time:

| | |
|---|---|
| Start-up | 10 minutes |
| Shut-down | 5 minutes |
| Total | 15 minutes |
| Work day | 480 minutes (8 hours) |
| Special Allowance | $\frac{15}{480} = 3\%$ |

**Standard Time**

Finally we arrive at the "standard time" for the job by adding all the allowances to the basic time:

$$\text{Basic time} \quad \begin{array}{l} + \text{ Personal allowance} \\ + \text{ Process allowance} \\ + \text{ Special allowance} \end{array} \quad = \text{Standard time}$$

Standard time, if correctly calculated will give you an accurate tool for comparing with results to measure productivity indices and for estimating and planning production; dividing the time per item into the minutes per hour will tell you how many can reasonably be expected per hour. It has other uses —

Stevedore labour loading cases of fruit into refrigerator ships had traditionally worked in gangs of four men, three gangs to a dockside crane. The crane landed a metal pallet of cases in the hatch and the men then removed them, carried and stacked them manually. It was very hard work.

A couple of years ago the shippers changed the method of shipment to pre-packed pallets which were dropped three at a time into the hold and then positioned by a forklift truck. The work of the men was now restricted to releasing the slinging mechanism when the pallets landed in the hold.

The shippers wanted not only to reduce the number of gangs to one, but also the size of the gang to two men. The men's union objected strongly to the breaking up of the traditional gang. However, after some discussion, it was agreed that a time study would be carried out jointly by the union and the shippers.

Once the study had been completed and the results tabled, it was clear to both parties that not only could two men easily perform the work but that, due to the long process time whilst the crane swung from ship to shore and back, they could service two cranes and still only have to work for 30% of available time.

The union accepted the study but asked for the provision of a third man as stand-by to relieve the other two when they went to "relieve" themselves. The shippers were happy to make this concession and the men got an easier and more productive job. Dealings with unions involving manning levels, rates, times and so on, are often made easier by a thorough knowledge of the job seen through the dial of a stop watch.

As you can see, assessing a standard time requires a fair amount of application and, as we said at the beginning of the chapter, we don't expect to see all managers rushing around with stop watches. However, we have found over many years of experience that simply exposing managers to the technique of time study greatly enhances their understanding of the job and the problems of productivity improvement. As such it's well worth the time involved.

**Things to remember**

● Even if not able to carry out work studies themselves, all managers should understand the basic technique of activity sampling, work sampling and time study because it will assist them in applying the work standards required of their employees.

● Activity sampling is a method of analysing the utilisation of manpower and machinery by making observations during the work period and recording what is happening at the precise moment of observation. These observations can then be summarised and expressed as a percentage of the total time.

● Work sampling is an extension of activity sampling in which the work produced during the period of observation is counted and a rate per unit of time calculated.

● The purpose of time study is to establish a standard time for a piece of work. The standard represents the time it should take an average, trained and motivated worker to do the work.

● The average time to complete an element or a complete job is known as "observed time" (OT). The rate at which the observed employee is working is compared to a performance standard (100) and allocated a "rating" (R) as a percentage of standard performance.

● Observed time is then corrected by multiplying it by the rating percentage, the result being the "basic time" for the job. Allowances for personal rest and relaxation, process time, and non-cyclic occurrences are added to basic time to arrive at a standard time for the job.

# Ways to improve productivity

We have spent some time discussing how productivity can be measured as a necessary prelude to its improvement and we have seen that often the process of measurement alone will indicate what must be done to correct or improve a position. However there will be many occasions when the fault and its remedy may not be so apparent.

It has been said of productivity improvement (as of many other exercises) that it is 10% inspiration and 90% perspiration. Inspiration certainly has its place in productivity improvement but, unfortunately, there is no way of escaping the perspiration involved in a methodical approach to the problem — so that is where we will start.

## Method Study

The first, and most common, approach to improving productivity is known as method study. It comprises a series of six steps which lead to the development of new and improved ways of doing a job.

- Challenge
- Analyse
- Question
- Develop
- Apply
- Measure

## Challenge

The first step in the method is to "Challenge the necessity of the operation" — is it really necessary for it to be done?

This may sound a bit presumptuous but you would be surprised how often asking such questions as "Why is it done? Is it really necessary?" and getting honest answers will uncover situations which perhaps were once necessary but are no longer.

It was a long standing instruction in the maintenance workshop of a large process plant that the bearings of every electric motor repaired in the shop would be renewed. This instruction was applied no matter how long the motor had been running since its installation or previous overhaul. The annual cost of replacement ran well into six figures.

After attending a productivity awareness course run by the company, the workshop manager decided to question the necessity of this automatic replacement. On investigation it appeared that the instruction had been issued several years before when the plant was operating to its full capacity and few of the operations had

stand-by motors. Today the position had changed considerably. Not only was the plant working well below capacity but also almost every key motor in the plant had a stand-by in case of failure and therefore stoppage through bearing failure would not affect the process.
He obtained approval to cancel the instruction and today only bearings which fail to pass a running test are changed. The cost of bearing replacement has been reduced by 75%.

**Analyse**

If the job is necessary and cannot be eliminated or combined with another then the next step is to analyse it.

First the job must be broken down into its elements and their sequence recorded. This can be done in several ways depending on the complexity of the job. Usually a simple listing of the elements will suffice but if the operation comprises several jobs, such as the making and assembly of a number of components, it will be necessary to draw a diagram showing the path followed by each component, the complete assembly or the person being studied.

To help you identify just what is being done in each element a simple code is used —

$\bigcirc$ = an operation

$\Rightarrow$ = the material or person moves

$\square$ = the item is checked

$D$ = work is delayed

$\bigtriangledown$ = the item is stored

The more operations there are in a job the longer it will take. The further the operator or material moves the more effort and time is required. Checking an item may be necessary to ensure quality but every inspection takes time. Delays are obvious time wasters whilst storage of finished or semi-finished products costs money.

Every element takes time to complete so a clear picture of the elements involved in any operation is a prerequisite to any attempt to change it. A detailed study will supply the evidence as to where utilisation and efficiency can be improved.

**Making tea**

◇ Take kettle to tap              *(2 metres)*

○ Fill kettle

◇ Return kettle                *(2 metres)*

○ Switch on

○ Lay tray

◇ Fetch milk                   *(4 metres)*

○ Put tea in pot

◗ Wait for kettle to boil

○ Fill tea pot

◗ Wait for tea to infuse

▢ Check before serving

A total of 5 operations, 12 metres of transportation, 2 long delays and an inspection — if you drank black coffee instead you would eliminate at least 4 elements!

## Question

Little boys tend to drive their mothers to near-insanity by continually asking, "Why, mummy?" of every topic and order raised. The mother's physical reaction to this irritant often leads the child to adopt an unquestioning acceptance of the status quo in later life, which may make a good citizen but makes a very bad method study person.

In order to improve productivity you need to cultivate an inquiring and sceptical mind which refuses to accept that there can't be a better way of doing things. To help you we suggest the use of a simple questioning routine based on Kipling's " — six honest serving men who taught me all I knew; their names are what and why and when, and how and where and who."

**?**

## QUESTION
## EVERY ELEMENT

| | |
|---|---|
| What is achieved? | Why is it necessary? |
| When is it done? | Why at that time? |
| Where is it done? | Why at that place? |
| Who does it? | Why that person? |
| How is it done? | Why that way? |

Frank answers to these challenging questions will lead you to consider ways of eliminating or combining elements, changing the sequence or timing of elements, changing the workplace or facilities, changing the person concerned or re-training them. The final question opens the door to improving and simplifying the method by reducing effort, movement and time.

### Develop

There is one place where inspiration will help considerably and that is in the development of a new method or way of doing things which will be an improvement in terms of utilisation, efficiency and overall productivity. This is also the place where "two heads are better than one", in fact the more "heads" you can involve in your search for improved methods, the more likely you are to come up with some original and effective solutions.

Over-familiarity with a situation can often prevent you from seeing it objectively, whilst "ego involvement" (being responsible for the present position) will act as a deterrent to thinking creatively about change. For these good and common reasons it is often helpful to use a brain-storming technique to develop new ways of doing things. The technique is well known but works well only if some simple but important rules are followed —

**BRAIN-STORMING**

- Choose participants with intelligence
- State objective clearly and restate frequently
- Record all suggestions no matter how far out
- Do not allow judgement or criticism
- Go for quantity

Once you have sufficient suggestions (at least 20) you can start to eliminate those that won't pass the test of the 4 R's — Do you have the *Resources* called for? Are there any *Restraints* which apply? What about the *Reaction* of other people/processes? What would be the *Result* of the suggestion — would it meet your objective?

The suggestions which pass this test can then be evaluated in terms of lowest cost, least amount of change, greatest improvement and so on, to arrive at the preferred new method.

## Apply

Now comes the real test of your ability when you apply the new method for the first time. Usually this is only done after the new method has been tried out and any snags eliminated. This can take quite a while, particularly if production is not to be affected.

If those concerned in the operation have participated in the development of the new method you should not have too much trouble in introducing it, provided you have dealt honestly with any objections or fears they have expressed. If the new method is to succeed it must benefit them as well as the organisation as a whole.

Worker benefits can include —

- Reduced effort
- Reduced anxiety or stress
- Increased interest
- Increased satisfaction
- Productivity bonuses
- Improved job security

If the operators have not participated in the development of the new method, no matter how small the change, it is vital that it be discussed in depth with them or their representatives before it is introduced. You should anticipate their fears that the change will make the job more demanding or that it will threaten their security in any way and be fully prepared to take whatever action is necessary to make the change acceptable to them.

Failure to gain their confidence at this stage can severely affect the improvement potential of the new method and can even, in bad cases, lead to an overall drop in productivity through non-co-operation by the operators. Even if you have their co-operation don't expect an immediate improvement — it takes time for people to learn new skills and to settle down. It is usually desirable to provide increased supervision and guidance during this period to speed up the settling down process.

## Measure

Assuming that you have safely overcome the application hurdle, the final step in method study is to measure the productivity of the new method and compare it with the old.

Did we say "the final step"? Of course, in productivity improvement there never is a "final step" because as soon as you have made an improvement you will want to start looking for other ways to improve. It's a never ending process.

## VALUE ANALYSIS

We have been talking about changing methods. There is a very similar technique for looking critically at the product itself — be it a physical item or a service. This is known as value analysis or value engineering. Its objective is to reduce the cost of a product without affecting its quality, ie its ability to perform its designated task.

In exactly the same way as a job is broken down into elements so a product is broken down into its components. The function and cost of each component is then analysed and items which show a potential for economy are selected for further study. Each component is subjected to a series of questions. Here are some of them —

- What function does it perform?
- Is its capacity greater than needed?
- Can it be made from another material?
- Can material wastage be reduced?
- Could a standard component be used?
- Can manufacturing tolerances be increased?
- How vital is the surface finish?
- Could the manpower and machinery content be reduced?

The next step is to create methods or designs which will achieve the desired economy. Finally the new product is tested to ensure that its function and value have not been impaired by the change.

A large multinational company which had imported all its machinery was in the habit of automatically ordering spare parts from overseas through the manufacturers. As a productivity project one of its engineers studied a sample of eighteen components and was able to source two-thirds of them locally at greatly reduced prices, leading to a saving in excess of R20 000 per annum.

One item in particular graphically illustrated the worth of value analysis. This was an igniter for an oil-fired furnace which cost in the region of R400 ex Europe. Careful examination of its function showed that it could be performed equally well by a standard motor-cycle spark plug costing R1,50 locally.

In these days of wildly fluctuating currency values such exercises become increasingly important if costs are to be contained.

Reducing costs by lowering standards is relatively easy and, in some cases, economically justifiable. Reducing costs without lowering standards is much more difficult but a necessary and important part of productivity improvement.

## Loss control

One of the questions raised in value analysis is whether wastage of material can be reduced. That question referred to a particular component under study. But of course, as we have seen in some earlier examples, since materials make up a major cost item in most products, the reduction or elimination of wastage will improve productivity.

Material is wasted in many ways as we saw in Chapter 3. Constant attention to the causes listed will ensure such losses are minimised.

One cause of loss not previously listed is that resulting from accidents. An accident causes damage to manpower, machinery and materials which has to be repaired or replaced at a cost in time and money — expenditure which is completely non-productive. Therefore any steps taken to avoid accidents by eliminating potential hazards can be justified in productivity terms.

Instituting a "safe working" programme alone may not do a great deal unless you have the whole-hearted co-operation of both supervisors and workers, both of whom have important roles to play. Workers are always tempted to short cut safety practices — safety helmets are hot and uncomfortable, monkey belts take time to put on and take off, machine guards slow down work cycles, and so on. This means that supervisors must always, and without exception, correct breaches of safety regulations. And workers must participate in drawing them up and in administering them.

Finally the C.E.O. must be seen to be a safety fanatic. Whenever he walks around his operation he should be on the lookout for breaches of safe working practices and draw these immediately to the attention of whoever is in charge. That way all the staff will know that the programme is for real.

## MOTIVATION

As we saw in Chapter 3, the cheapest way to increase productivity is to improve motivation. However, whilst it is cheap, it certainly isn't easy, particularly in these days of burgeoning and highly politicised unions.

Before the recent growth of the trade union movement, supervisors used to be taught how to build and maintain good human relations with their workers, and were shown how eliminating the demotivators and supplying them with the motivators they needed could increase their job satisfaction and productivity.

Nowadays the emphasis seems to be solely on teaching supervisors how to apply disciplinary and grievance procedures, and how to protect themselves when accused of unfair labour practices. This change of emphasis has caused many supervisors to alter their perception of the labour force from co-workers to adversaries.

As has long since been discovered in heavily unionised industries overseas, the presence of an active union does not preclude the participation of workers in decisions which affect them (worker participation does not mean management abdication). Nor does it hinder the setting of clear responsibilities and the essential feedback of progress towards objectives. It does not prevent the restructuring of jobs to make them more interesting and rewarding. Neither does it prohibit any organisation from allowing workers to share in the monetary benefits of increased productivity.

Any or all of the above will improve employee motivation (at any level). Motivated employees are generally less likely to take industrial action than unmotivated, dissatisfied employees.

Given the tremendous difference in output between motivated and unmotivated employees perhaps it is time we considered the advantages of a pro-active attitude towards motivation as opposed to the potential productivity losses stemming from a re-active attitude towards workers' demands.

## REDUNDANCY

In the minds of many workers productivity and redundancy are synonymous. Unfortunately their belief is often reinforced by the ill-considered utterings of management who link the two in public statements and private behaviour which the unions are quick to exploit.

It would help if the use of the word "redundancy" were restricted to the side effects of a reduction in production for whatever cause — shrinking or lost markets, recessions, downturns and so on. When these occur it is necessary to reduce the work force proportionately so that the organisation may retain its profitability and thus protect the jobs of the survivors (layoffs in the motor industry are a typical example of redundancy at work). Increased productivity seldom results since the potential capacity of the organisation is no longer being fully utilised.

On the other hand the objective of productivity improvement is to increase production and/or reduce costs (of which only one element is labour). Improving a product's ability to compete in the market will usually increase demand thus increasing its sales and creating more job opportunities. In the few cases where method improvement creates surplus staff these can usually be retrained and employed in the additional work thus created. If they do have to be separated there should be adequate funds stemming from the improved contributions to ensure they are generously treated.

One thing is certain and that is that mixing a redundancy programme and a productivity improvement programme is fatal to the latter. The advice of those who have tried it and suffered is clear — get rid of your surplus staff before trying to improve the productivity of those who are left.

## THINGS TO REMEMBER

● Any steps which improve utilisation and efficiency of resources will improve productivity.

● The most common approach to productivity improvement is method study. This comprises six steps which first challenge the necessity of the operation and then analyse its elements in detail as a necessary preliminary to developing and applying a new method.

● The objective of value analysis is to reduce the cost of a product without affecting its quality. It follows a similar questioning routine to method study concentrating on specific components of the product.

● Safeguarding materials from loss or damage can make an important contribution to productivity as can the elimination of loss or damage to all resources due to accidents by means of a "safe working" programme.

● Greater emphasis on the motivation of employees by their supervisors will pay big dividends in increased productivity.

● Care should be taken not to confuse or integrate redundancy programmes with productivity improvement programmes.

# How to measure and improve clerical productivity

**6**

Our overview of productivity measurement has so far concentrated on the operational activities involved in manufacturing and service industries — the physical activities which produce products and which can be determined and measured relatively easily. We have deliberately avoided the area of clerical activity which supports such operations.

In most Western countries the number of people employed in the so-called "white collar jobs" far exceeds those in traditional "blue collar" jobs. As our bureaucracy grows, so in this country too, we are reaching the same position. Yet, with a few exceptions such as major banks and similar enterprises, little has been done to measure, monitor and improve the productivity of clerical workers in a majority of South African organisations.

Those organisations that have attempted the task, like their industrial colleagues, have either employed specialist study personnel or have brought in consultants. In doing so they have run into the same distrust of standards and resistance to change which seem to beset such interventions.

It is not necessary to bring in specialists to measure clerical productivity or to improve it. It can be, and should be, made a part of every supervisor's job — just as we have shown can be done in any operational situation. The key to the whole programme is to encourage the participation of the staff themselves in both measurement and improvement. The method we are about to describe involves the department manager, the section supervisors and staff members. We will look at the role of each separately starting with the most important people in any productivity programme — the staff who are going to be affected.

Obviously before starting on a program of this nature it would be necessary to inform the staff and also to train them in what they are expected to do. We will be dealing with both of these aspects in a later chapter. In the meantime let's assume they are all ready to start.

## Defining tasks

You have learned so far that the first step in any measurement process is to define what is being measured. In the case of activity sampling and time study you reduced all jobs to "elements" for measurement purposes. You have to do the same thing in clerical productivity measurement except that elements of clerical work are usually referred to as "tasks".

So the first step is to get all staff members to draw up a list of the tasks which comprise their jobs. Preferably this should be done in conjunction with their section supervisors who must ensure that all tasks in the section are covered by one or more employees' lists. Generally the staffer will have a job-description or a work list covering his or her job and this should describe the tasks. If, as is likely, the job description is out of date, now is the time to update it. If a job description doesn't exist this would be a good time to draw one up, preferably in conjunction with the staffer concerned.

## Measuring clerical utilisation

The same factors affecting manpower and machinery which we discussed in Chapter 3 are equally applicable to clerical work. Thus in any programme for increasing productivity your first job is to measure the utilisation of your staff and machines.

Provided the tasks can be visually determined it is possible to do this by activity sampling using the technique we explained in Chapter 4. However, in many clerical operations it is difficult to see precisely what is being done ("thinking" can't be seen nor its objective determined by an observer). For this reason it has been found preferable to encourage the staff members to measure their own work.

This method, although not as accurate as professional activity sampling, has many advantages. It allows the staffer to participate in the programme at an early stage. It creates an awareness of time-wasting activities. It highlights areas where productivity can be improved and develops an understanding of why measurement is so valuable.

Utilisation can be measured very easily by having the employees keep a daily diary or log of how their time is spent. The basis of the log is a matrix with the hours of the day running across the top and the minutes per hour down the side like this —

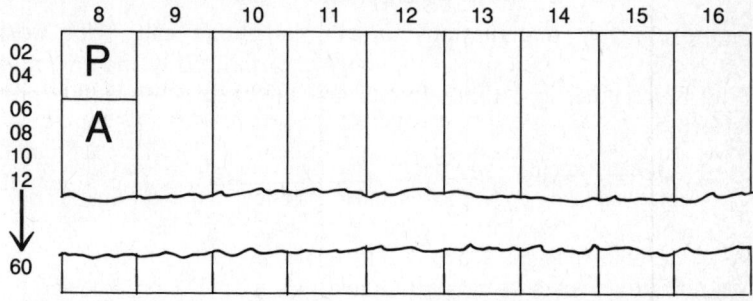

The employee and supervisor then devise a simple code to cover both *productive time* (agreed tasks) and *non-productive* time, such as waiting for work, interruptions, phone, walking, rest and so on. To complete the log the employee blocks in the time spent on each activity during the day as it is completed and identifies it with a code letter.

In the example above the employee spent from 0800 to 0805 using the telephone (code "P") and then went on to task "A" (whatever that might be). At the end of the day the time blocks are added by codes and then separated into productive and non-productive time. The total of the two should equal the official working hours, whilst the productive time expressed as a percentage of working hours will indicate the utilisation being achieved.

$$\frac{\text{Total productive time} \times 100}{\text{Official working hours}} = Utilisation$$

The number of days needed to give an accurate picture of the job will depend on its nature. If the job is cyclical (ie if the work varies from day to day or week to week) it will be necessary to log sufficient days to capture all the normal cycles. If the job involves roughly the same work each day, four or five days will be sufficient.

Analysis of these simple logs can provide a great deal of valuable information which can help the employee to avoid lost time and extra work.

### CAUSES OF LOST TIME

- Poor work planning
- Inadequate facilities
- Information search
- Non-productive interruptions
- Productive interruptions

*Non-productive* interruptions include telephone calls (not work-connected) and socialising. *Productive interruptions* include meetings (and more meetings!) both formal and informal — particularly the latter.

A senior executive was once asked by a consultant how much of his time was taken up by meetings. He said he didn't know but thought it was about 30%. The consultant suggested he get his secretary to keep a log for him for a few days.
At the end of three days his secretary gave him this breakdown:

| | |
|---|---|
| Formal meetings with colleagues | 5% |
| Formal meetings with subordinates | 7% |
| Formal meetings with clients, etc | 6% |
| Informal meetings with colleagues | 9% |
| Informal meetings with subordinates | 23% |
| Informal meetings with clients, etc | 5% |
| | 55% |

The consultant suggested that he investigate why it was necessary for his subordinates to take up so much of his time (30%). It could be lack of delegation or training or both. If he could reduce this time he would not only increase their productive time but also be able to spend more of his own time with clients or on other more productive responsibilities, such as planning or controlling.

The executive was so shaken by the result that he cancelled all his meetings for that day and spent the time planning how he could improve his delegation to reduce time-wasting informal meetings."

The final step in measuring utilisation is for the staff member to draw up a *task list* recording the tasks in order of importance together with the percentage each forms of the total work load, the factor which influences the volume of work and the monthly work volume.

| TASK LIST | | | | |
|---|---|---|---|---|
| No. | Name: J. B. SMIT<br>Dept.: ACCOUNTS<br><br>Task | %<br>Total<br>Work<br>Load | Control factor | Monthly<br>Volume |
| 1 | CHECK SUPPLIERS I/V's | 30 | PURCHASE ORDERS | ± 3000 |
| 2 | PREPARE PAYMENT SLIPS | 5 | INVOICES | ± 500 |

The "percentage of total work load" can be estimated from the time logs already prepared by the staff members. The "control factor" is whatever influences the work load (eg the more purchase orders issued, the more invoices received) and is helpful when planning and balancing work loads, as is the "monthly volume" figure. The completed task lists are collected by the supervisor who needs them for the analysis of the total work load he will carry out later.

**Measuring clerical efficiency**

Clerical efficiency (ie the time taken to complete a given task accurately) can be measured by time study in just the same way as other work. However it can be disturbing for the employees who also may not accept the time standards resulting from it. Here too it is preferable to let them participate by timing themselves.

It has been found in practice that employees will generally try to give an accurate assessment and, in any case, any attempt to "cook the books" can be spotted fairly easily by comparing one staffer's time with another's.

The first step is for the employee to agree with the supervisor on the task to be studied and how many items are to be timed. The staffer then selects a batch of items representing between 10 and 30 minutes of work and proceeds to work through them recording the time started and time finished for each item. Tasks taking longer than 30 minutes should, if possible, be broken down into several, shorter segments. Interruptions must be excluded from these times as these have already been measured by the "time-log" procedure.

| WORK SHEET | | | | |
|---|---|---|---|---|
| Name: J. SMiT Dept.: ACCOUNTS | | TASK Checking supplier's I/V's | | |
| | ITEM | | TIME | |
| No. | Reference | Started | Finished | Taken |
| 1 | CLACK + Co   2478 | 0900 | 0906 | 6 |
| 2 | CLACK + Co   2479 | 0907 | 0912 | 5 |

It is essential that the staffers fill in the worksheet as they go along so that the times are factual and not "guesstimated". After a little practice they will be able to do this without unduly affecting their normal work. As and when they have a few minutes of spare time they can summarise the forms and pass them on to their supervisor.

| | | | | |
|---|---|---|---|---|
| No. of items | 10 | Total time taken | 65 | |
| | | Av. time per item | 6,5 | |
| Signed: J. Smit | | add Allowance - 16,7% | 1,1 | |
| Checked: BRT | | Standard Time | 7,6 | |

The allowance of 16,7% (or 10 minutes per hour) is an accepted allowance to cover rest and relaxation for clerical workers and is added to the average time per item to arrive at a standard time per item for that task.

You will probably find that their first lists will contain some items which took an exceptionally long time. Rather than increase the number of studies in an attempt to reduce the deviation to 30%, the easiest way to handle them is to treat them as separate tasks (eg long invoices and short invoices).

As the staff members complete their studies they will start to compare their actual times with the standards they have given to their supervisors and will work out for themselves what their daily targets should be. They will start to think about ways to improve productivity and, if you really get lucky, they might even ask you for more work!

## Putting the measurements to work

It will take several weeks to collect standard times for all the clerical jobs in a section but once these have been completed you have the raw material for a powerful productivity measurement tool which will enable you to measure the productivity index of a section, a department or the whole administration function of an organisation.

The first step is to group tasks by activities (eg all the tasks which make up the payroll activity) and calculate the monthly total time required for each task.

$$\frac{\text{Monthly Volume} \times \text{Standard Time}}{60} = \textbf{Monthly total time (hrs)}$$

Adding the monthly totals for each task making up an activity will give you the total time (standard time) that should be spent on that activity per month. Similarly, adding up all the activity times will give you the total workload for the section, department or organisation expressed in hours of work or "manhours" as we prefer to call them.

You can find the number of hours actually worked by simply multiplying the number of staff employed by the hours they should work per month. Comparing this with the standard manhours that should have been worked will give you a productivity index for the operation.

$$\textbf{Clerical productivity index} = \frac{\text{Total standard manhours} \times 100}{\text{Manhours actually worked}}$$

If you want to translate this result into numbers of people all you have to do is divide the total standard manhours by the number of hours in

59

a working month to find how many people you should have (A) and compare this with the number you actually do have (B).

If "A" is bigger than "B", show the figures to your boss and suggest that it is time you were suitably rewarded. If, as is more likely, "B" is bigger than "A" on no account let your boss see the figures until you have a plan to improve them, so that, like all successful managers, you can present him with the problem and the solution at the same time. If he's not impressed you can always become a consultant!

## Improving clerical productivity

The basic methods of work study and improvement discussed in the previous chapter apply equally well to clerical work, ie breaking work down, challenging each step, eliminating or combining work and developing new methods. The major difference is that in this area we believe the employees should be trained and encouraged to carry out their own studies and suggest improved methods.

The reasoning behind this is threefold. Firstly, they are closest to the actual work and therefore often know of bottlenecks and problems which are hidden from the supervisor — a file drawer which jams, a temperamental photostat machine, etc. Secondly, if their ideas are accepted they will want to see them successful and will work towards that end, thus probably ensuring their success and the ensuing saving. Thirdly, analysing their work and developing new methods gives them a new interest in their jobs, improving their overall motivation.

One day the management of a large laundry introduced an employee suggestion scheme with cash prizes for the most productive suggestions. It was well supported and a number of worthwhile entries were received.

In due course the managing director presented the prizes in the staff canteen. First prize went to an elderly woman who had been with the company for many years and who had suggested a novel and efficient way of sorting coloured and white garments during reception which would save the company many thousands of rands. When the managing director presented her with her prize he remarked, "I suppose this idea of yours is a result of the many years of experience you have had in your job?". "Oh, no sir!" she replied, "I got this idea ten years ago when I first joined the company but no one has ever asked me before".

Earlier on we gave you five **causes of lost time.** Here are some remedies:

**CAUSE**

| Poor work planning |
| --- |

**REMEDY**

- Eliminate bottlenecks
- Balance work load (after measurement)
- Eliminate cyclical peaks

In most offices the end of the calendar month is a good time to go off sick! Invariably the staff is expected to handle 30-40% of the monthly work load over 3 or 4 days. Mistakes are made, tempers fray, machines break down. Productivity suffers.

There are many ways of eliminating these peaks such as staggering returns and deadlines. One highly successful method is to work a 13 month year — each "month" exactly four weeks long. This moves the heat off the calendar month end and, as a side effect, provides exactly comparable periods for productivity and performance statistics. In fact all it needs is for the problem to be identified and many solutions will be suggested.

**CAUSE**

| Inadequate facilities |
| --- |

**REMEDY**

- Re-schedule work
- Re-allocate equipment
- Increase capacity

In many offices today the problem is often to fully utilise the equipment provided rather than the inadequacy of facilities. Where such a problem does exist it can often be overcome be re-scheduling work so that everyone doesn't need the computer terminal or adding machine at the same time. Re-allocating facilities such as space may often be necessary and, as a last resort, increasing capacities may be justified if it results in a greater increase in productivity.

| CAUSE | REMEDY |
|---|---|
| Information search | ● Re-locate information source<br>● Improve filing efficiency |

Studies indicate that much time is wasted searching for information needed to process work. A careful study of time lost in this manner may indicate the value of updating the information filing and retrieval processes.

| CAUSE | REMEDY |
|---|---|
| Non-productive interruptions | ● Keep phone calls brief<br>● Discourage socialising |

Once you start to measure clerical time in a time-log you will become painfully aware of the vast amounts of time lost in phone calls. First of all it interrupts the work flow and this takes time to get moving again. Then there is the time wasted in saying "Hello" and "Goodbye" and the endless repetitions of questions and answers. If you want a rude shock, attach a tape recorder to your phone for a day and play it back at the end of the day. You've never heard so much useless garbage in your life! It is possible to be brief and to the point without being rude and it's a style that should be cultivated.

One thing that should not be cultivated is socialising, gossiping or whatever it's called in your office. Every office has its share of gossips but the trouble is they waste two people's time, theirs and that of the people they trap. This can add up to quite a few manhours by the end of the day.

| CAUSE | REMEDY |
|---|---|
| Productive interruptions | ● Avoid unplanned meetings<br>● Keep planned meetings short |

Calling an unplanned meeting on the spur of the moment means that, apart from you, the other participants will be unprepared and therefore unable to give their best contribution. It also means that those attending will not have had time to re-schedule their work and are therefore probably holding up the work flow of others. The effect cascades down through the organisation.

Allowing subordinates to call on you at any time (the once popular "ever open door") will wreck your own work scheduling.

> A busy and successful executive developed an effective method of reducing the length and frequency of time-wasting interruptions by both colleagues and subordinates without keeping his door shut. If anyone came to see him without a prior appointment he would stand up to greet him and remain standing until the visitor left. Since the visitor could scarcely sit whilst he was standing the interviews were usually brief and their frequency reduced, their place being taken by pre-planned meetings which fitted the work schedule of both parties.

There are many films and books about the time wasting capability of planned meetings. They all emphasise four basic rules —

### RULES OF MEETINGS

*ALWAYS*
- Draw up written objectives (ie results to be achieved)
- Set a start and finish time and stick to them.
- Distribute an agenda ahead of the meeting.
- Keep a written record of results achieved.

Writing out the meeting objectives will force you to describe accurately the results you expect to achieve and setting time goals will at least limit the amount of time you will have wasted if you don't achieve them.

The agenda not only sets the priorities for discussion, it also gives all those attending the responsibility of preparing thoroughly. A written record of results will provide sombre evidence of your success or failure in running a productive meeting.

### Keeping it going

The novelty of a productivity measurement and improvement programme conducted by the employees themselves will ensure a flow of productivity improvement suggestions for some time but, unless artificially stimulated, this flow will dry up and they will slowly return to the bad old habits. Some ways to keep it going are:

- Group projects
- Job re-structuring
- Client/supplier relationship
- Brain-storming problems
- Regular reviews

Giving a small group of employees a *problem to investigate* and solve helps to keep their creative juices flowing and renews their interest in productivity — it also takes a load off the supervisor.

Some thought can be given to *re-structuring jobs* to increase responsibility and interest. Allowing people to check their own work is one way of achieving this which leads to the establishment of *client/supplier relationships* — the staff member supplies output material to another staff member (client) in another section or department, instead of pooling the output and supplying it to an unidentified client section or department. Personalising the relationship in this way increases the feeling of responsibility and job interest.

Often asking the staff (agenda) to participate in a planned (timed) *brain-storming meeting* to resolve a section or department problem (objective) will provide an excellent opportunity to rekindle their enthusiasm for productivity improvement.

Finally, a regular *review of workloads* by re-measuring tasks will provide a constant incentive towards productivity improvement.

## THINGS TO REMEMBER

● The measurement and improvement of clerical productivity should be a part of every supervisor's job and should involve the staff members doing the work.

● Before starting to measure clerical productivity it is necessary to break all the work done in the department or section into tasks.

● Utilisation of the clerical work force can be measured by having each staff member keep a time-log for a number of days. Analysing the time-log will highlight where time is being wasted.

● The easiest way to establish the workload in a section, department or organisation is to have each staff member measure the time taken to complete a number of batches of work, item by item.

● These times can be averaged to give an average per item to which is added an allowance of 16,7% for rest and relaxation. The resultant figure is the Standard Time per item.

● Multiplying the standard time by the number of items handled per month will give the total time allowed on each task per month. Adding the results for all tasks and dividing this figure by the official working hours per month will indicate how many employees are required to handle the work load. This figure can be compared with the actual numbers employed and will highlight areas where improvement is needed.

● The best source of ideas for improving work methods is the staff members themselves who should follow the basic techniques for method improvement already given.

# Profit from productivity

**7**

Although we have discussed in some detail the measurement and improvement of productivity in three of the four principal resources, we have deliberately left to last the most important resource of all without which nothing happens, namely "money".

Obviously, when productivity of the other three resources is improved, costs are reduced or production increased, or both. This will increase their contribution to the organisation's finances. But whether the increased contribution will result in increased profit will ultimately depend on whether the organisation's finances are fully utilised and efficiently managed. Indeed, improved utilisation and efficiency of the money resource may often show even greater potential for productivity improvement than the other resources.

But before those of you not presently working within the finance or accounting division of your firm decide that all this stuff about money doesn't apply to you, let's be quite clear about something — the money resource is managed every single day by every single employee in the firm. How can we justify such a claim?

Well, the organisation's funds are ploughed either into the production process in order to make products to sell, or into the supplies and expenses incurred in keeping the process going. Only when the products (or services) have been finally paid for by the customers does any of the money come back into the firm's hands in the form of profit.

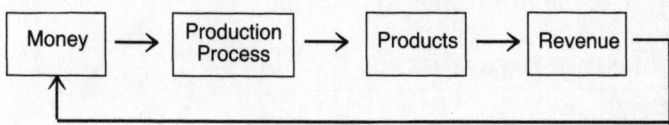

The longer it takes for the money resource to work its way through the system to become available for reinvestment, the harder it is for the firm to be profitable. As we will show, everyone in the organisation directly or indirectly affects the overall productivity of the money resource at the end of the day and all these employees can thus help to improve that productivity. At every level managers should be aware that all the facilities under their control are a part of the total money resource. How well they manage them individually will ultimately add up to how profitable the whole organisation becomes.

Now that we have reassured you that this chapter is certainly not for the accounting boffins only, let's discuss how we go about measuring the utilisation and efficiency of the money resource.

**Measurement of input**

The money resource consists of those things in the organisation in which capital has been invested in order to make money — commonly terms "assets". They are usually categorised into "fixed" assets and "current" assets, and some managers may be more involved with one type of asset than another.

67

What is important is that they are recognised as investments which require an adequate return on them to justify their existence. If they are not earning an attractive enough return, or worse still if they are actually losing money, the firm may as well wind itself up and the shareholders put their money in a bank or building society where they will receive a safe and steady return on their investment without having to lose sleep at night worrying about it.

## Fixed assets

Fixed assets in most organisations comprise those items which are bought with a view to holding and using them for a relatively long period of time. They include buildings, plant and machinery, furniture and fittings and motor vehicles. The firm acquires them because it needs them in order to produce the goods or services it wants to sell.

There are two vital factors which will affect how productive the funds invested in fixed assets will turn out —

**PRODUCTIVITY OF FIXED ASSETS**

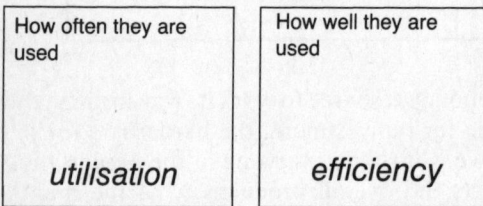

It is easy to see that a heavy truck working 18 hours a day will produce a better return on its original investment than one that works only 10 hours per day provided they are both efficiently operated. It is perhaps less easy to see that installing a mezzanine floor in a warehouse could materially increase its return on investment also.

To calculate the input figure for the measurement of fixed asset productivity you need first to total the value of the assets under your personal management. Although there are many ways in which fixed assets can be valued depending on the end use of the figures, for productivity measurement it is usual to use the original cost of each item as a basis and this figure should be readily available.

## Current assets

In addition to the money invested in fixed assets there is the money which is used to keep the production and marketing process running from day to day, usually known as current assets.

This includes money tied up in stocks of raw materials, work still in progress, stocks of finished products, customer credit, and the cash you keep on hand to meet the innumerable expenses of administering a business concern — wages and salaries, electricity, rent, water, postage, stationery and so on. In many service operations and smaller firms, where heavy capital equipment is not necessary, the current assets can be far larger than the fixed assets.

The bad news is that an adequate return must also be earned from this portion of the money resource which is not even generally recognised as an asset by those using it. Once money is poured into current assets, it is in fact "dead money" since no interest or return will result until the goods or services are sold for a profit.

The secrets of high productivity of current assets are —

**PRODUCTIVITY OF CURRENT ASSETS**

| Keep investment as low as possible | Turn investment over as quickly as possible. |
|---|---|

The longer it takes for the money resource to work its way through the system the more has to be pumped into the system before sales pop out at the other end.

Two small businesses are making the same article and have the same basic costs per week —

| | |
|---|---|
| Raw materials | R1 000 |
| Labour | R 500 |
| Overheads | R 500 |
| Total | R2 000 |

and sell the article for R3 000.

Business 'A' takes one week to produce the article which it sells for cash the following week. Its production/sales cycle is two weeks long and therefore it has to invest R4 000 in order to sell R3 000 worth of goods at a profit of R1 000, a return of 25% on its investment every week.

Business 'B' takes 2 weeks to produce the article which it sells on credit 6 weeks later. Its production/sales cycle is 8 weeks and so it has to invest R16 000 in order to sell the same R3 000 worth of goods at a profit of R1 000, a return of only 6,25% on its investment every week — which isn't to be sneezed at but is not as good as Company 'A'.''

## Return on assets managed (ROAM)

There are many ways in which the profitability of an organisation can be measured. The one which best demonstrates the productivity of a section, department or total operation is the Return on Assets Managed.

**PRODUCTIVITY OF FIXED ASSETS**

$$\frac{\text{Contribution (Sales — Costs)}}{\text{Total Assets (Fixed + Current)}} = \text{R.O.A.M.}$$

ROAM simply measures the output in monetary terms as a percentage of the total assets employed in the department, branch or organisation being measured. Most commonly, the output figure is the contribution of the division, etc., calculated by subtracting the cost of goods sold from the gross sales income.

The percentage return can then be compared to a standard set by management and a Productivity Index for the money resource can be calculated. This will indicate the need for action.

## Analysing sub-standard P.I.'s

If your ROAM PI is less than 100 there are a number of other measures which will help you pin-point which specific portion of the assets is being least productively managed.

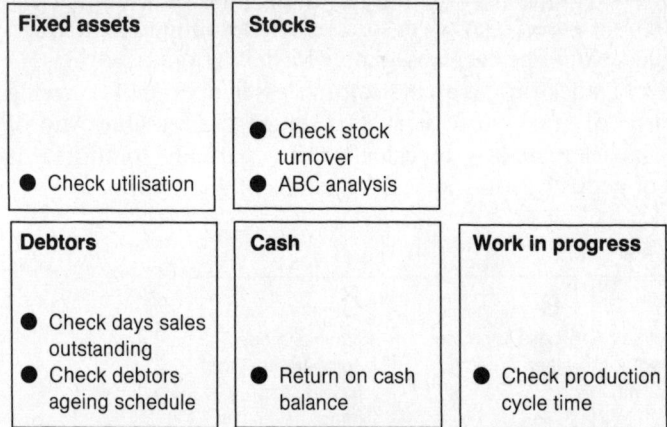

| Fixed assets | Stocks |
|---|---|
| ● Check utilisation | ● Check stock turnover<br>● ABC analysis |

| Debtors | Cash | Work in progress |
|---|---|---|
| ● Check days sales outstanding<br>● Check debtors ageing schedule | ● Return on cash balance | ● Check production cycle time |

Generally a regular review of the utilisation of fixed assets will reveal those that are not being used to capacity and action to correct the position can be initiated.

As far as current assets are concerned, you will need to use measures which will tell you how long the money resource is taking to move through the production/selling cycle. The longer it is taking, when measured against your own historic figures or against an industry norm, the lower your return on assets will be, as we have seen. If you have no idea as to the normal ratios for your type of business most of them are available from the Bureau of Financial Analysis at Pretoria University.

## Measuring stock turnover

In a number of industries, the bulk of working capital is invested in stock, be it in raw materials, work in progress or finished goods. The most useful ratio for measuring your stock management is the stock turnover ratio or "stock turn" as it is known —

$$\frac{\text{Cost of goods sold}}{\text{Average inventory}} = \textbf{Stock turn}$$

Average inventory is calculated by averaging the opening and closing stock figures for the period you are measuring. The ideal stock turn figures will differ substantially from industry to industry. In an industry such as a supermarket where profit margins are low, stock is expected to turn over very rapidly during the year (10-12 times). On the other hand, one would expect a far lower stock turn in an antique shop where profit margins would be correspondingly higher.

The value of stock turn as an indicator is less in operations carrying a wide range of stock since it is an average figure. One way of improving its usefulness is to calculate it separately for different categories of goods by using an ABC analysis of your stocks.

**ABC ANALYSIS**

| **A** | **B** | **C** |
|---|---|---|
| Items generating highest proportion of sales or profit. | Less important than A items. | Minimal money spinners held to provide a full range. |

Generally category A items will account for about 70% of turnover, whilst B and C together bring in the other 30%. For this reason more attention must be paid to regular turnover analysis and measurements in A items than in the other two.

**Measuring debtor levels**

Credit facilities can certainly play a part in boosting sales. But what you need to keep a tight control over is whether the extra sales are in fact contributing to a better return on assets, or whether they are diluting it because the extra customers take too long to pay up (or end up not paying at all).

You need to know on a frequent and regular basis how long your debtors take to settle their accounts. An analysis of "Days sales outstanding" will tell you —

$$\frac{\text{Total debtors} \times \text{Selling days in month}}{\text{Monthly credit sales}} = \textbf{Day's sales outstanding}$$

The standard you set will depend on the type of business you operate. Generally businesses which offer 30 days terms try to keep their average outstanding below 45 days, and use a simple ageing schedule to pinpoint the accounts that require attention.

These days all business will try to extend the period of payment because it is a cheap way to borrow money. Only constant monitoring of debtors' records will tell you whether their delays are within acceptable limits or whether they are diluting your own resource productivity.

## Measuring cash utilisation

In these days of high inflation, any idle cash sitting around in a till or in a low interest account is actually losing money for the company. Measuring the interest you receive on your annual average cash balance and comparing it with the best the money market can offer will tell you whether or not your cash management is dragging down your overall return on assets managed.

A consultant, reviewing the monthly accounts of a large service operation with branches in all the major centres, noted that the 'cash-on-hand' figure exceeded R1 million.

He remarked on the size of this figure to the Managing Director who admitted that it was high but said that it had improved since the previous year. He said that his accountant had assured him it was not a problem and was only a side-effect of the branches' efforts to increase collections at the month end to show a better figure for 'days sales outstanding' which he had been hammering recently. This resulted in a large inflow of cash which was held to meet salaries and other month-end expenses, the surplus being transferred to Head Office a week later.

The consultant demonstrated that R1 million at only 15% interest could earn R400 per day which was at present being lost to the company. He suggested a revised method of cash flow forecasting for the branches and overnight transmissions of funds into selected accounts.

Within three months the average cash-on-hand total had dropped to R50 000 and interest on cash invested was steadily building up.

## Improving the productivity of assets

You will have noticed that in our approach to the productivity of assets we have followed the same path as we used in the case of the other resources, namely, to measure before attempting to improve.

Some of the measurements themselves indicated where and how improvements could be made. In addition there are a number of well-tried methods which you can use.

## Fixed assets

The approach here is to ensure you acquire the correct assets in the first place and then ensure they are fully utilised thereafter.

### Acquisition

- Assess alternatives using a financial technique such as discounted cash flow.

- Biggest is not always best — buy the most suitable asset for the job.

- Consider alternatives to purchase, like leasing, to conserve capital and avoid obsolescence.

- Always consider cost of repairing before replacing.

### Utilisation

- Use to full capacity. If you can't use them fully consider letting out to other companies.

- Train employees to use assets efficiently and maintain them correctly.

- In a high tech environment, plan ahead so that systems are compatible.

Acquisition decisions are made by senior management but using the assets is everybody's job. They should be aware of the contribution they can make to improved productivity.

## Current assets

In the case of current assets all employees are involved and need to know how they can help.

### Improving Stock Management

- Use a technique like "economic order quantity" to ensure that initial purchases of goods are kept to a minimum quantity.
- Try to reduce lead time involved in ordering goods to reduce stock holdings.

- Try to reduce or eliminate safety stock by changing to reliable suppliers.
- Avoid obsolete stock by keeping your finger on market trends.
- Use discounting to move dead stock.
- Fully utilise creditor financing — buy for cash only when discounts obviously pay.
- Ensure that sales, production, buying and despatch work together to get goods to the customer as fast as possible.
- Keep tight control on stocks lost by shrinkage (by staff as well as customers).

The job of tightening up on the amount of money tied up in debtors is not purely that of the credit department or the credit controller. Rather it involves a broad policy approach which gives firm guidance to all the employees concerned as to what the allowable terms are and how they should be enforced.

The newly appointed financial director of a large service company was horrified to see the extent of funds tied up in debtors, particularly in their main branch operation. This branch handled over 50% of their business but its debtors averaged 67 days' sales outstanding.

He called the branch managers together and demonstrated to them how the excessive sums required to service debtors was affecting their profitability as well as exposing them to bad debt losses. He set as a target 45 days' sales outstanding and together they drew up a plan to achieve it.

First of all each branch manager would appoint a smart and presentable member of the staff as credit controller. He would then visit each client, introduce the creditor controller and explain diplomatically that economic conditions had forced them to apply a more rigid credit policy. He would also explain that the credit controller would be in constant touch with the client to ensure there were no queries or problems which might hold up payment beyond the thirty days allowed.

The credit controller would ensure that invoices were issued immediately a job had been completed and that statements were mailed on the last day of the month. He would then follow up from the 15th of the month to ensure they had arrived, were free of error and ultimately to ask for payment. If this failed to produce payment within 40 days the branch manager and the credit controller would call on the client and request payment.

Within five months of installing the procedure the days' sales outstanding for the company was within target and the main branch was running at a phenomenal 39 days. More than $\frac{3}{4}$ million rand was released for other, more profitable investment.

Ultimately, cash management is about making your spare cash work as hard as possible for you all the time, and the first part of that process is speeding up the collection of cash owed to you. The second side to efficient cash management involves earning the best possible interest on temporarily idle amounts which inevitably accumulate. As we have seen this demands accurate cash flow forecasts so that you can anticipate when surplus funds will be available for investment and when they will be needed again for business operations.

Once you know how much you have to invest at any one time, you should investigate what is the most attractive investment that will match your needs, ie match the greatest accessibility with the best interest. Your bank manager will have plenty of advice on such investments, and a small computer programme can make cash forecasting and management much more efficient.

Finally, as we have seen, a poorly planned production process can tie up large amounts of cash in "work in progress" (WIP). Speeding up the process through the application of work study and reducing line stocks of raw material and semi-finished components will have a marked effect on the cash tied up in WIP.

In service industries the costs involved from the time a job starts until it is invoiced is in fact work in progress although it is seldom recorded as such. Delay in completing a job and delay in invoicing after completion can both increase WIP and action to reduce such delays will release more cash into the business.

**The bottom line**

It is no good being interested in productivity improvement without ultimately being able to measure its impact on the bottom line — net profit. For improving productivity is not about working harder, it's about working smarter. And the only way you will know whether it is paying off or not is to look at the return on the money resource of the company. ROAM really is the bottom line measurement as to whether your productivity programme is working or not.

76

## POINTS TO REMEMBER

- The management of the money resource is not purely the concern of the financial division — it concerns every employee.

- The money resource is ploughed into fixed and current assets, which must be productively used to produce an adequate return.

- The measurement of money productivity is the "return on assets managed".

- If the return is inadequate there are other measurements which focus on the productivity of each type of asset. These include utilisation of fixed assets, stock turn ratio, days' sales outstanding, and the return on cash balances.

- The utilisation and efficiency with which fixed assets are used determines their productivity.

- The productivity of current assets depends on how fast the money resource can be moved through the production and selling process, thus limiting the amount of "dead money" in the system.

- Productivity improvement must be measurable in terms of its effect on the profitability of the company. This is done by constantly measuring the return earned on the money resource employed as Return on Assets Managed.

# Setting up a productivity programme

# 8

Where should we start? At the top? In the middle? At the bottom? There are many theories as to the best place to focus the programme and there's a grain of truth in each of them.

| | |
|---|---|
| **Top Management** | Some maintain that the programme must be imposed on the organisation by top management who are the only people who know the organisation's strategic objectives and can therefore channel the effort where it will have the greatest effect. |
| **Middle Management** | Others believe that only middle management has the authority to get things done combined with sufficient knowledge of the workface to know where to look. |
| **Supervision** | Since the supervisors are in closest touch with the job and, in any case, will have to implement the changes, the programme should be focused on them. |
| **Workers** | The workers actually do the work and therefore they are in the best position to suggest improvements. |

All these approaches have been tried with varying degrees of success. The two extremes have been found to be the most difficult to implement. Programmes handed down by top management tend to arouse resistance in middle and lower management leading to a less than 100% commitment.

Although some success has been achieved with worker controlled programmes such as the American "Quality of work life" and the Japanese "Quality circles", they generally require a dedication and common interest which are unfortunately lacking from our scene. In addition the individual worker's view of resource utilisation and efficiency is severely restricted to his/her own workplace and thus the projects produced seldom tap the real potential.

Long experience in the introduction of productivity improvement programmes indicates that the best and fastest results come from those focused on middle management with active support from top management and a planned filtering down to the supervision level once the programme has been established. The introduction should follow these steps —

- Gain management commitment
- Select and train team leaders
- Form and train teams
- Choose the projects
- Maintain progress

## Gaining Commitment

Some time back we said that the most important person in any attempt to improve productivity was the employee or operator involved in the process. We would like to change our minds on that one, or at least add another name, and that is the Chief Executive of the organisation.

It has been our unhappy experience that unless the CEO is both enthusiastic and committed to the need for an ongoing productivity programme you are going to waste an awful lot of time and energy trying to get one going. It isn't necessary for him to take a direct part in the programme but it is vital that he keeps a fatherly eye on his divisional managers' efforts, and that he is seen by the staff generally to be wholly behind the programme.

A large manufacturing plant split its management into operations, engineering, technical and administrative divisions under a CEO who reported to a Board of Directors. The managers of the divisions were strong, well-qualified individuals who each sincerely believed that the success of the operation rested on his shoulders alone. This attitude permeated down through the divisions creating
relationship problems in the various departments of the plant.
After attending a symposium on productivity improvement the manager of the engineering division, having obtained the CEO's reluctant approval, asked consultants to set up a productivity improvement programme. This they did by selecting a small group of engineers and exposing them to the basic principles of measurement and improvement in a training course. After the course the participants formed themselves into a small committee and worked on a number of productivity projects.
These proved highly successful so that further courses were arranged until a total of 50 engineers and foremen had been trained and formed into departmental teams with projects totalling more than R2 million.
At this point, the operations manager, who had played no part in the

programme, decided to introduce an overseas system of progress reporting by which each department would be treated as a separate cost-centre and would be responsible for setting itself cost-cutting objectives. Although it was pointed out to the CEO that this exercise would divert effort from the productivity programme, he declined to interfere.

Within six months the number of productivity teams shrank to four and the projected savings by 75%; the cost-centre exercise failed to take its place.

How do you get commitment from the CEO and his management team? The easiest way is to give them copies of this little book and make sure they read it. Failing that you will have to prepare a presentation (based on the book) stressing the need for measurement and improvement in your organisation. If you want it to be really effective, take the time to work out a couple of productivity measures and show the monetary effect of a possible 5 or 10% improvement compared with the cost of introducing the programme. Since the figures involved are likely to be substantial this should arouse some interest and make gaining commitment easier.

You should also take the opportunity to outline the roles of the CEO and his team, and gain their full acceptance of the parts they must play —

**MANAGEMENT ROLES**
- Announce the programme to the staff.
- Decide on incentives (if any).
- Monitor overall progress.
- Recognise outstanding achievements.

Whatever you do, don't make the mistake of starting a programme without their commitment.

### Selecting Team Leaders

Bearing in mind that the team members are going to be drawn from middle and lower management, team leaders should be chosen from senior management. If your organisation is large enough to justify departmental teams then it would be natural for department managers to act as team leaders thereby ensuring their full participation. However in smaller companies, where several departments could be represented in the team, the leader should be chosen for his knowledge of the subject and ability to hold the respect of the team. Very often a training manager will fill this function well.

Team leaders should agree on their responsibilities and should be given an overall target to aim for —

### RESPONSIBILITIES OF TEAM LEADER
- Approve projects against agreed criteria.
- Hold regular meetings with team to ensure progress of projects.
- Co-ordinate outside assistance if required.
- Obtain necessary authority for projects.
- Encourage development of lower level teams.

The criteria with which approved projects must comply will include such items as ensuring that the project is worthwhile in time and effort; that it addresses a recognised problem; that it is tabled in an acceptable form; that it includes progress deadlines which must be met.

It is important that productivity team meetings are kept separate from other meetings otherwise the recurrent crises of normal business will cause productivity to be shunted aside as less important. The meetings provide an opportunity for brain-storming of solutions to difficult problems and generally help to keep enthusiasm at a high level.

Sometimes a team member may need technical or specialist help in researching a project. The team leader ensures it is available. He also obtains approval from higher authority for projects which are beyond his limits.

As the team gains confidence it's the leader's job to encourage the secondment of supervisors and lower level managers onto the team so that there is as much participation as possible.

In order to do the job properly the team leaders should be exposed to a modified version of the training given to team members so that they can reinforce the vital points of measurement and improvement.

### Forming and Training Teams

The composition of the productivity teams will depend on how big you are. If you are big enough to form departmental teams (from four to ten members per team) you will do better than if you have to select individuals from each department and make them into a team. But don't let this stop you — you'll still gain tremendous benefit from individuals.

**COMPLEX PROJECTS MAY REQUIRE MORE MEMBERS**

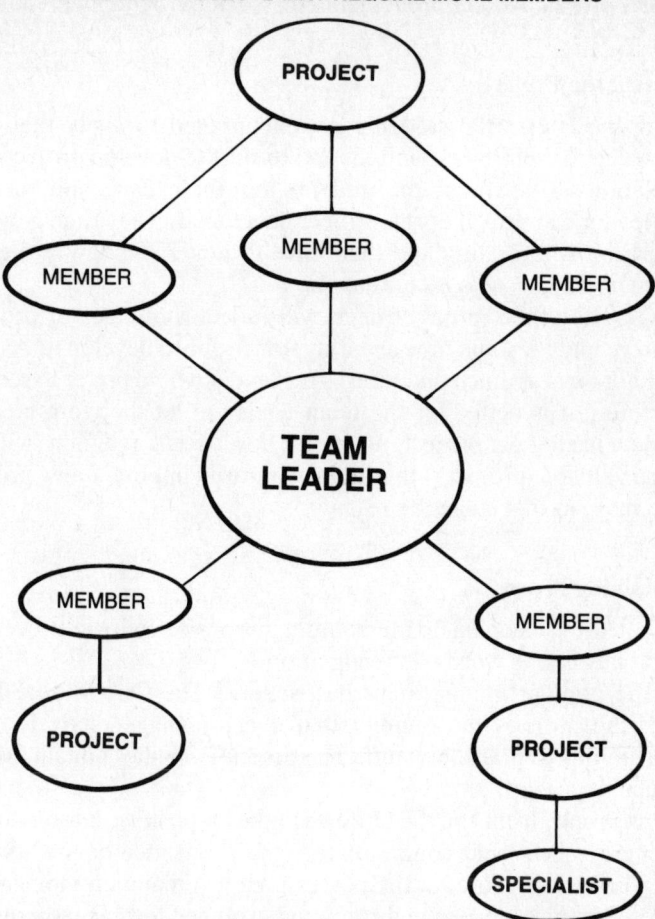

If you have a training officer or department they can put together a productivity awareness course using the material in the book supplemented with examples from your own business. Alternatively there are ready-made A/V packages available and a number of consultants who will put together and present courses for you.

The usual duration is about three days which can be spread over a week to make release of participants from their jobs a little easier. The members of each course should be drawn from as many departments as possible to help cross-pollination of ideas and also to underline the fact that productivity improvement crosses departmental boundaries.

## Choosing the Projects

During the course the students are encouraged to apply their new knowledge to their own situations and to start to develop projects. On completion of the course the students join their teams and get their team leader's approval of the project developed. They then continue to work on it to finality and then have to develop a new project to replace it. The process is continuous.

Quite often their initial projects will reflect some idea or problem they have had for some time awaiting some spur to develop it. As such it may not have as much potential as the leader would prefer to see. We have found it is better for the team leader to let the team member complete his/her pet project, no matter how trivial, and then switch to a more valuable project rather than arbitrarily impose a new project, which may, at that stage, be resented.

## Maintaining Progress

The real key to keeping up momentum in a productivity improvement project lies in one word — "recognition".

In the popular management best-seller, "The One-Minute Manager", the authors recommend that every manager actively seeks opportunities to praise his staff. The principle applies equally well to productivity teams.

If everyone, from the CEO down, takes a positive interest in the ongoing projects, and congratulates teams and members who complete worthwhile projects, the programme will maintain momentum. Some companies have gone further and arranged formal gatherings at which praise and rewards are given for successful projects. The rewards need not be substantial; the fact that the individual or team effort has been recognised is much more important.

## The Payout

Training and running the productivity teams costs money so what sort of payout can you expect in return? Here are some first-year results —

| Company | Team Members | Increased Productivity |
|---|---|---|
| Sugar Company | 17 | R400 000 |
| Oil refinery | 65 | R3 000 000 |
| Packaging Company | 17 | R700 000 |

The average of those savings ranges from R23 000 to R46 000 per team member and figures of that order of magnitude are not uncommon. Of course the figures will depend on how much scope there is for improvement. If you already have a highly efficient organisation and are monitoring productivity carefully you may not achieve such high results. On the other hand you might just be surprised!

What we are really saying is that the possible benefits so heavily outweigh the small costs involved that the only sensible decision that has to be made is not, "Should we introduce the programme?" but rather, "What is the earliest date that we can make a start?"

Why not make it tomorrow?

## THINGS TO REMEMBER

● Experience has shown that the best place to start a productivity improvement programme is with middle managers.

● Without the full and visible commitment of top management a productivity programme will fail.

● Team leaders should be selected from department managers and their responsibilities agreed on prior to commencement of the programme.

● The teams themselves can be any size from 4 to 10 members. Larger teams are difficult to co-ordinate.

- The training of teams can readily be carried out in-house using this book as a basis, supplemented with practical examples.
- Team members will develop projects as a part of their training.
- Recognition of results is a key to keeping the programme alive, well and producing.
- Payout from a properly run programme should exceed R20 000 per team member.